Patrick Hunter Thoms

An Account of the Morgan Hospital

With a Sketch of the Morgans of Dundee, The Scheme for the Erection and

Endowment of the hospital, and the Regulations for its Fovernment

Patrick Hunter Thoms

An Account of the Morgan Hospital
*With a Sketch of the Morgans of Dundee, The Scheme for the Erection and
Endowment of the hospital, and the Regulations for its Fovernment*

ISBN/EAN: 9783337163167

Printed in Europe, USA, Canada, Australia, Japan

Cover: Foto ©Andreas Hilbeck / pixelio.de

More available books at **www.hansebooks.com**

MORGAN HOSPITAL

AN ACCOUNT

OF THE

MORGAN HOSPITAL,

WITH A SKETCH OF

THE MORGANS OF DUNDEE,

THE SCHEME FOR

THE ERECTION AND ENDOWMENT OF THE HOSPITAL,

AND THE

REGULATIONS FOR ITS GOVERNMENT.

DUNDEE:

PRINTED BY JAMES P. MATHEW & CO., MEADOWSIDE.

1870.

CONTENTS.

THE MORGAN HOSPITAL.

THE story of the MORGAN HOSPITAL may be told in few words. Mr JOHN MORGAN, whose name it bears, and through whose munificence the funds for its erection and endowment were provided, died at Edinburgh on the 25th August 1850. On the death of his last surviving sister, Miss AGNES MORGAN, which took place on the 15th January 1848, certain writings were found in her repositories, executed by her brother, containing some personal bequests of small amount, and declaring it to be his wish that the bulk of his fortune should be employed to establish in Dundee, the place of his nativity, an institution for the education of boys on the model of Heriot's Hospital in Edinburgh. Previously to the death of his sister, Mr MORGAN had fallen into a state of mental imbecility, and a *curator bonis* was appointed by the Court of Session to take the management of his affairs. The writings alluded to passed into the hands of the *curator.* Having learnt their import, the Magistrates and Town Council of Dundee were naturally desirous of ascertaining their validity as testamentary deeds. It was known that Mr MORGAN had left a large fortune. Various parties came forward claiming to be "nearest of kin" to the deceased, and it soon became evident that their conflicting claims would not be settled without the intervention of judicial authority. For the better understanding of these writings, extracts from them will be found in the Appendix.*

Special mention is made of the Nine Incorporated Trades

* Appendix No. I.

of Dundee in one of the papers found in Miss MORGAN'S repositories, and a Memorial was submitted by them for the opinion of counsel in regard to their rights under the deeds referred to. That opinion was unfavourable, and, in consequence, no further steps were taken by the Nine Trades at that time. The Magistrates likewise resolved to take the opinion of counsel as to the effect of the writings executed by Mr MORGAN. A Memorial was accordingly prepared and laid before eminent counsel, a copy of which and of the opinion is given in the Appendix. *

It will be observed, that, whilst admitting the difficulty attending the questions as to the validity and effect of these writings, counsel held it to be the duty of the Memorialists (the Magistrates of Dundee) to watch over the competition which was likely to ensue as to the general or residuary interest in Mr MORGAN'S succession, and to take the proper time for putting forward a claim, under the bequest, before the fund was divided or otherwise disposed of. Upon this advice the Magistrates acted, and, during a prolonged litigation betwixt two sets of claimants for the succession, in the course of which two Appeals were successively taken to the House of Lords from the judgments of the Court of Session, they took no further steps, but continued to watch the proceedings in the competition. After the case had, under the second Appeal, been again remitted to the Court of Session, it seemed probable that an arrangement would be entered into betwixt the litigants, and it then became necessary to put forward the claim of the Town of Dundee to prevent the division of the funds until that claim should be disposed of.

Up to that time no active steps had been taken to vindicate the claim of the Town, but Mr GEORGE ROUGH, who was then

* Appendix No. II.

Provost of the Burgh, and Mr DAVID HUME, Convener of the Nine Trades, both of whom took a deep interest in the case, along with those gentlemen who had been originally engaged in the investigation of the writings left by Mr MORGAN, resolved to convene a meeting of parties known to be friendly to the cause of education, for the purpose of considering the position of matters, and deciding upon the measures which should be adopted to support the claim of Dundee to the benefit which it was clearly the intention of Mr MORGAN to confer upon the town.

A meeting was accordingly held in the Town Hall, on Wednesday, the 17th October 1855, which was numerously attended; and at the meeting Mr JAMES DODDS, Parliamentary Solicitor, London, who had been consulted by the Magistrates as to the case, was present, and gave a luminous exposition of its legal bearings, shewing that whatever might be the fate of an application to the Courts in Scotland, the result of an Appeal to the House of Lords would, in his opinion, be "eminently hopeful." The meeting was unanimous and enthusiastic in its determination to maintain the claim of the community of Dundee, under the writings left by Mr MORGAN. Resolutions to that effect were passed, and a Committee was appointed to carry out the objects of these resolutions.* A subscription was opened, and a sum, amounting to upwards of £800, was promptly subscribed, to meet the requisite expenses of judicial proceedings. One half of the sum subscribed was called up to meet the costs of the proceedings now to be detailed.†

* Appendix No. III.

† By the judgment of the House of Lords, the Appellants—the Town Council and Nine Incorporated Trades of Dundee—were found entitled to their expenses. The subscriptions were consequently repaid to the subscribers, under

Without narrating the various steps of the procedure in the
Court of Session, it may be enough to state that an action
of Multiplepoinding, as it is termed, having been raised by
the judicial factor who had been appointed to administer Mr
Morgan's Estate, and being still in dependence before the
Court, a petition was presented, in name of the Magistrates
and Town Council, and of the Convener and Boxmaster of the
Nine Trades, for liberty to appear in this action, as having
an interest in the succession. The Court of Session, on
the 2d February 1856, refused the petition, with expenses;
but, at the same time, indicated an opinion that the proper
way of testing the validity of the writings founded on by the
Petitioners was by an Action of Declarator, to which those
claiming to be the "nearest of kin" should be called as parties.
Acting on this suggestion, an Action of Declarator was
accordingly raised in name of the Town Council and Trades ;
but the competency of such an action was denied by the
other parties. A debate took place, and an Interlocutor
was, on the 17th December 1856, pronounced by the judges,
who were unanimous in sustaining the competency of the
procedure. This implied no deliverance on the merits of
the case, and, after a record had been made up and counsel
heard, the Lord Ordinary, on the 29th May 1857, pronounced
an Interlocutor disallowing the claim of the Town of Dundee,
and dismissing the action with costs. The case was carried
by Reclaiming Note before the Inner House (Second Division), and here again, after a debate, a judgment adverse

deduction of a small sum for extra-judical expenses which was not recovered
under the judgment.

It is due to the professional gentlemen—Counsel, Agents, and Parliamentary
Solicitors, by whom the case for the Town of Dundee was so ably conducted—
to state that they offered to give their services gratuitously in the event of its
being unsuccessful.

to the claims of Dundee was pronounced on the 26th June 1857.*

Up to this point the result of the proceedings in Court was disheartening, and now, when it became necessary to call up the remaining half of the sums subscribed, some of the subscribers regarded the issue as hopeless, and declined to pay the last moiety of their subscriptions. The Committee, however, to whom the management of the case was confided, were prepared for an adverse judgment in the Court of Session, and resolved not to abandon the claims of Dundee until the judgment of the tribunal of last resort should have been obtained, and the case was carried by Appeal to the House of Lords.

In compliance with the rules of that House, a case was lodged for the Magistrates and Town Council of Dundee and the Nine Incorporated Trades, and counsel were heard for the parties on the 25th, 26th, 29th, and 30th days of March 1858, but judgment was not given by the Lords until the 11th May 1858.† By that judgment the Appeal was sustained; the writings executed by Mr MORGAN were found to be good and effectual testamentary writings, and to "contain a valid legacy and bequest of so much of the personal estate of the said testator, JOHN MORGAN, as is necessary to found an Hospital in the town of Dundee, to accommodate one hundred boys;" and it was remitted to the Court of Session to carry the judgment into effect, and to frame a scheme for the establishment and regulation of the Hospital.

After protracted discussions in the Court of Session, judgment was, on the 8th February 1861, pronounced, with the consent of parties, whereby it was found that the sum of

* Appendix No. IV. † Appendix No. V.

£73,500* should be paid by the executors of Mr MORGAN for the establishment and support of the Hospital. Previously to this a voluminous case was prepared for the Town of Dundee, shewing the expense of maintaining boys in various hospitals and charitable institutions, and statements in opposition were likewise brought forward by the praties claiming the executry of Mr MORGAN. To guide the Court in fixing upon the sum requisite for the Hospital, a remit was made to Professor CAMPBELL SWINTON to prepare a scheme for the erection and endowment of the Hospital, and also for the government of the institution after the building should have been erected. The scheme prepared by Professor CAMPBELL SWINTON received the sanction of the Court, and forms the constitution under which the Hospital is now conducted. The scheme is printed along with this narrative.

The result of the proceedings in the courts of law fully justified the course pursued by those who, in the face of disheartening indifference and opposition, deemed it due to the memory of Mr MORGAN, as well as to the community of Dundee, not to abandon the case until it had been carried to the ultimate tribunal.

The accounts of the successful issue of the Appeal to the House of Lords were received in Dundee with public demonstrations of joy, and the efforts of those who were entrusted with the superintendence of the litigation were rewarded by the result. It would be ungrateful not to acknowledge the exertions of the professional gentlemen—counsel and agents—which led to that result. A meeting of the subscribers to the fund for sustaining the Town's claim, and of the friends of education, was held in the Town Hall of Dundee on the 17th

* Appendix No. X.

May 1858,* and resolutions were passed expressive of the satisfaction felt by the meeting, and their sense of the valuable service rendered by the gentlemen who directed the proceedings.

After the appointment of Trustees and Governors in terms of the judgment by the Court and of the scheme sanctioned by it, measures were taken for the erection of the Hospital. A site was acquired on the Estate of Craigie, lying to the north-east of the town, and a plan, prepared by Messrs PEDDIE & KINNEAR, Architects, Edinburgh, was approved of and adopted by the Governors.

The foundation-stone of the edifice was laid with Masonic honours by the Earl of DALHOUSIE, Lord-Lieutenant of the County, and Grand Master for Scotland, on the 30th July 1863. Unexpected causes of delay retarded the progress and completion of the work; but it was so far finished by the close of the year 1867 as to admit of the Hospital being opened for the reception of boys. It was formally opened on the 5th February 1868. By that time a Head Master and other officials had been appointed, and forty boys had been received into the House. Since that period successive additions to the number have been made, and eighty boys have now (May 1870) been admitted to the benefits of the Institution. Whether it will be in the power of the Governors to receive a larger number will depend in a great measure on the income which may be derived from the money invested for the support of the Establishment.

For the satisfaction of those who may desire information as to the personal history of Mr MORGAN, the founder of the Hospital, and of his family, reference is made to the Address delivered by the writer of this narrative at the opening of

* Appendix No. VI.

the House, on the 5th February 1868, which forms a sequel to
this statement. The writer was Chief Magistrate of Dundee
at the time of Mr MORGAN's death. He was delegated by the
Magistrates to obtain the opinion of counsel for their guidance. He was likewise nominated as Convener of the Committee for directing the proceedings for the vindication of the
claim of the Town of Dundee under the testamentary writings
of Mr MORGAN. Hence he was led to watch the proceedings,
and acquired an intimate knowledge of the case, as well
as of the history of Mr MORGAN's family. To render the
narrative complete, and to preserve an account of the proceedings taken to secure for the town the benefit of the
bequest by Mr MORGAN, reference is made to the various
documents and reports of the meetings alluded to, which will
be found in the Appendix to this memoir. The case in its progress and its issue is regarded by Scottish jurists as a *cause
celebre*. It terminated in the application of the true principle of interpretation to testamentary writings—namely,
the ascertainment of the intention of the testator in devis-
ing his effects—a principle consonant with justice, and
opposed to a system which rested mainly on the formalities
and subtleties of law.

P. H. T.

SKETCH OF THE MORGANS OF DUNDEE:

AN ADDRESS

Delivered at the Opening of the Morgan Hospital,
on Wednesday, the 5th February 1868,

By PATRICK HUNTER THOMS, Esq. of Aberlemno.

When a stranger approaches the building in which we are now assembled [the Morgan Hospital], after expressing his admiration of the structure, his first enquiry will naturally be, For what specific object is the Hospital designed? and the next, What is the history of the individual whose name it bears, and by whose generosity the funds destined for the erection of the building and the endowment of the Hospital have been provided? To the first subject of enquiry it may be answered in the words of the scheme sanctioned and approved of by the Court of Session, by interlocutor dated 8th February 1861, that this Hospital has been established " for the education, lodging, boarding, and clothing of 100 boys, the sons of tradesmen, mechanics, and persons of the working class generally, whose parents stand in need of assistance to enable them to educate their families, or who are orphans in need of such assistance." It is farther provided by the scheme, that during the first year after the building is completed and ready to be inhabited not more than forty boys shall be admitted. Out of the applicants for admission the Governors, after the most anxious consideration of their several claims, selected the prescribed number of boys. These you have seen to-day, and I am sure you will unite with me when I give expression to the hope, that they will prove themselves deserving of the preference shown them, by attention to the instructions which they will receive within these walls, and by a career of useful and honourable conduct when they go forth into the world. In regard to the second branch of the enquiry, having been led by circumstances which I need not at present detail to take a special interest in the bequest of Mr John Morgan, and to watch the proceedings which terminated in establishing the claim of the Town of Dundee to so much of the personal estate of Mr Morgan as was, according to the judgment of the House of Lords, required for the endowment of the Hospital, I endeavoured to collect from the various sources to which I had access the particulars of Mr Morgan's history, and that of the family to which he belonged. These particulars are embodied in the following sketch, which I shall now, in compliance with the desire of the Governors, proceed to lay before this meeting of the friends of the Hospital.

Our story commences a few years after the middle of the last century, and the scene of it is laid in the Royal Burgh of Dundee. At this period the town contained some 10,000 or 12,000 inhabitants. The march of improvement had scarcely begun in Dundee. The ancient cross stood on an elevated platform on the High Street. The Town House and spire, from a design by the elder Adam, had been finished only a few years before. The Old Kirk occupied the site of the present East Church, but excepting it, and the Tower or Old Steeple, together with a portion of the transept which formed the South Church, the magnificent pile of buildings, which is said to have been erected by the Earl of Huntingdon about the beginning of the thirteenth century, lay in ruins. The Kirk Yard, or space around the churches, was unenclosed. On the east side of this space was a range of houses, to one of which I shall have occasion more particularly to allude. In taking his morning walk towards the Shore—for so the Harbour, or all that could be called a Harbour, was designated — the indweller of Argyllgate (now known as the Overgate) has to pass through the Kirk Yard ; and as he brushes along, he is hailed by a stout, fair-complexioned man, who leans over a half-door (or wicket) with shirt-sleeves rolled up, having a comfortable woollen nightcap on his head, and a voluminous apron wrapped round his waist, and who invites him, according to a custom then prevalent, to take a draught of his ale. The brewer now before us is Thomas Morgan. The house which he occupied, after undergoing various changes, has recently been converted into the elegant Restaurant known as the Café Royal, in Tally Street. About two years previous to this Thomas had begun business, and already had acquired the reputation of being a thriving maltman. To share in his prosperity and add to his comfort, he had a few months before taken unto himself a wife. He was married on the 1st December 1757 to Janet Cramond, who is reputed to have been a woman of strong good sense, and greatly devoted to the care of her family and household. If talent be hereditary, that possessed by the Morgans was doubtless a heritage of their mother. John Morgan, the father of Thomas Morgan, was married to Euphan or Euphemia Dakers or Dacres, while he was tenant of Mains of Gardyne, in the parish of Kirkden. This was about the year 1708. He removed from this farm to Seaton, parish of St Vigeans, in 1718. It appears that he did not remain long there, for he removed to Ravensby, in the parish of Barry, about 1726, and we find him residing at Wallace Craigie, Dundee, in 1728.* John died a few years thereafter, and his widow took possession of a cottage in the parish of Carmyllie, which was destroyed by fire on the 20th May 1737. Thomas himself, it is belived, was born at Ravensby in 1726 or 1727, but the precise date of his birth has not been ascertained. Thomas Morgan was respected by his neighbours, and in the evenings his tap or public room was usually filled by the more respectable citizens, who repaired thither, after the booths were closed, to speculate on the news of the day, and talk over anything remarkable which had occurred in the town or neighbourhood. The exploits of the year 1745 were comparatively recent, and generally formed the staple of conversation, when other topics failed. Many anecdotes were preserved of the hairbreadth escapes of Prince Charles, and the unswerving fidelity of the chieftains who supported his cause. It is even said, that occasionally at these meetings,

* John Morgan became unfortunate, and was incarcerated for debt, as we find from a disposition executed by him in favour of David Gardyn of Latoun, on "all and haill his outsight and insight plenishing." The narrative bears, "Forasmuch as I am presently incarcerate within the Tolbooth of Dundie," and the deed is dated 7th May 1729 years.

when the mirth waxed loud, toasts were drunk to "him that's far awa'," and songs sung in praise of "the lad we daurna name." Newspapers were at this period almost unknown in Dundee. A stray number of the *Caledonian Mercury* or *Evening Courant*, published in Edinburgh, occasionally found its way to Dundee, and supplied food for conversation to the quidnuncs of the town. It was usually deposited in the shop of James Stark, the bookseller—for Dundee then had only one bookseller—whose stock-in-trade included not only bibles, catechisms, school-books, and stationery, but also an assortment of wax-dolls, hand-balls, and Dutch toys—and, as James was on very friendly terms with Thomas Morgan, the newspaper generally found its way, in the course of a few days, to the taproom in the Kirkyard. On such occasions the Burgh schoolmaster, who lived hard by, was usually called in to read the tiny sheet, and also came in for a round of invitations to tea—tea was then a luxury—that he might retail the news which he had gleaned from the columns of the Edinburgh newspaper.

We need not dwell on the customs of those times. As already mentioned, Thomas Morgan was looked upon as a thriving man. His family increased. Three of his children —two sons and one daughter—died in childhood or early life; but he had two sons and three daughters who grew up, remarkable for their stature and for the energy of character which distinguished them. John Morgan, the second son— the eldest died in infancy—was born on the 28th February 1760. Thomas, a younger brother, was born on the 18th March 1764. At this period Dundee presented little scope for commercial enterprise, and there was slight inducement for young men who had nothing to rely upon but their own talents and industry to settle in the town. Thomas Morgan gave his sons the best education which the Burgh and Grammar Schools could afford, and they were distinguished among the youth of the place by the staidness of their conduct and a desire to improve their position, as well as by a certain measure of reserve, which their companions attributed to pride or self-importance. John, having completed a six years' course of attendance at the Grammar School, was sent to a writer's office, where he sharpened his pens and his wits at the same time. Here he acquired a smattering of law, which may have proved useful to him on some occasions, but which probably furnished the real cause of that length-ened litigation which terminated in the dedication of the greater part of his fortune, in virtue of certain writings exe-cuted by him, to the erection of the Morgan Hospital in Dundee. We are, however, outrunning the progress of our narrative. Thomas Morgan, the second surviving son, was articled as an apprentice to a Doctor—that is, one who com-bined the practice of physic and surgery with the dispensing and sale of medicines. In the year 1779 we find the name of "Thomas Morgan" entered as a matriculated student of anatomy and surgery in the University of Edinburgh. At this particular time India was regarded as the garden of the Hesperides, or the land of golden promise. Accounts almost fabulous reached this country of the gems and spices of that distant territory. The subjugation of successive native Princes and the additions made to the dominions of the East India Company, increased the military reputation of Great Britain, and attracted to the Company's service young men fired with a spirit of enterprise or military ardour. To that inviting land both our young townsmen directed their longing eyes. Thomas succeeded in obtaining the appoint-ment of assistant-surgeon in the service of the East India Company, and John obtained license from the Directors to proceed to Bengal as a free merchant. Through what influence the Morgans obtained those privileges we are unable to tell, but we know that George Dempster of Dunnichen, who sat in Parliament as the representative of this district of burghs—for Dundee had till the year 1832 only a fraction of a member—himself a native of this town, was ever ready to lend a helping hand to deserving young men who applied for his advice or assistance, and it is thought that he did so in the case of our two youthful townsmen. Be this as it may, in the year 1780, or soon after, both the youths quitted their native place to push their fortunes in a distant land, of which at that time little was known which could be relied on. We now lose sight of them for a number of years, and return to the honest malt-man in the Kirk Wynd, whose circumstances soon underwent a change for the worse. Thomas Morgan was reputed an honest trader. Some said he was too honest. This could not be; but Thomas either made his ale and beer too good, or he was too remiss and unsuspecting in his dealings; and the result was, that, after striving in vain to keep his head above water, he fell into embarrassed circumstances, was evicted from his brewseat, and, after struggling for some years, was necessitated to execute a trust deed, conveying his estate in favour of certain parties as trustees for behoof of his creditors. Thomas shifted his residence, but he continued to retail malt-liquors, assuming for his new house the sign of the Royal Oak. Here, although he enjoyed the respect of his acquaintances, and the sympathy of those who knew him in better days, his trade did not prosper, and he sunk into poverty, and died in August 1799. Thomas is now in his grave. The spot is marked by a tombstone erected in the Howff or Old Burying Ground here in the year 1817 to his memory by his son John, after his return from India—a proof that, though his name had ceased to be turned over by former neighbours and acquaintances, his son cherished the remembrance of his kindness and solicitude for the welfare of his family.* Whilst the two sons of Thomas Morgan were pursuing their respective callings in India, the daughters were industriously employed at home. As dressmakers and milliners they carried on business, and were enabled not only to earn a livelihood for themselves, but to contribute towards the support of their aged parents. Indeed, it was upon the fruit of their labours that, during the later years of his life, Thomas Morgan depended almost entirely for the means of subsistence. Some entries in the books of the Maltmen Fraternity show that he received donations from their funds. We do not call these donations charities, because Thomas contributed towards the funds of the Incorporation, and thereby purchased a right to relief from them when the cold hand of poverty came down upon him. He had at this period three daughters; one of them died about the beginning of the present century. The survivors, Matilda and Agnes, strove honourably and successfully to maintain their position. They wrought with their

* Appendix No. VII.

hands, but they kept up their hearts; and they would some-
times excite the wonder of their friends by telling them about
their brothers, when, at long intervals, letters came from them
with tidings of their success. Here we may mention that
John, after spending some years in mercantile business in
Calcutta, went into the interior, and became an indigo planter.
He was attentive and successful. His brother Thomas seems
to have forsaken the medical profession, and to have joined
his brother in the cultivation and sale of indigo. There
appears, indeed, to have existed a strong attachment betwixt
the two brothers, and their fortunes and history were united
until they were separated by the death of Thomas in the
year 1815. We have said that letters from their brothers
told the sisters of their welfare and prosperity. These letters
by-and-bye contained substantial proofs of their continued
concern for the members of their family whom they left behind them. Remittances were sent home by the absent
brothers—small at first, but subsequently of larger amount—
to provide for the comfort of the old people, and to aid the
sisters in their honourable exertions to maintain their position. But this was not all. Fortune had begun to shower
her golden favours upon the planters of the east. The two
sisters now relinquished their business, being supplied with
ample means of subsistence for themselves and their aged
mother by their absent brothers. Whispers were circulated
that the two nabobs were about to return to their native
country; and at last it was announced that they were preparing to quit India with a large fortune.

It was in June 1812 that John and Thomas Morgan
appeared in Dundee. The mansion of Balgay had been
engaged for them, and there they continued to live with
their mother and two surviving sisters nearly three years.
Many of the old friends of their father's family repaired to
Balgay to express their good wishes, and offer to the
Messieurs Morgan congratulations on their return to the
place of their nativity under circumstances so auspicious.
Truth compels us to say that, whatever may have been the
motive, such visits were, generally speaking, not well received; and, on the elevation which they had attained, they
seemed willing to forget the humble level from which they

had raised themselves. It may be that the artificial state of society in which they had so long moved, and the habit of reserve which they had acquired, induced them to keep aloof from intercourse with the inhabitants of Dundee ; but this was felt by their mother and sisters to be a great privation, and was probably the cause of their removal to Edinburgh, where their wealth would enable them to obtain admission to circles more congenial to their taste. There is, in truth, little worthy of remark in connection with the residence of the Morgans at Balgay. Their attention was at that period much occupied with the realizing of their property in India, and the remitting of the proceeds to this country. Even at this time, however, it is said, on the authority of Miss Agnes Morgan, that her brothers, as they walked amidst the grounds of Balgay, spoke of the difficulties attending their own early progress in life, and their desire to do something which should at once perpetuate the name of their family, and smooth the ascent of their youthful townsmen to respectability and honour. After transferring their residence to Edinburgh, the Morgans lived for a time in the neighbourhood of Haddington. They returned, however, after a short interval, to Edinburgh, and there passed the remainder of their lives. It may be here mentioned that Thomas Morgan (the younger) died at Haddington on the 13th August 1815 ; that the mother of the Morgans died at Edinburgh on the 14th October 1818 ; and that Miss Matilda Morgan died there on the 20th March 1827 ; Miss Agnes Morgan died at Edinburgh on the 15th January 1848 ; and John Morgan, who must be considered as the leading subject of this sketch, died on the 25th of August 1850, in the ninety-first year of his age.* The merits of John and Thomas Morgan were of no ordinary kind. They could boast no advantage of birth or connections. They fought the battle of life bravely and well. No whisper was breathed to their discredit in regard to their dealings in a land where in former times men were not remarkably scrupulous in matters of business or morality. Their deep-seated attachment to their parents and sisters formed a distinguishing and estimable trait of their characters. But, doubtless, they had

* Appendix No. VII.

their failings ; and of these the most remarkable in men of such vigorous minds was a desire by all means to connect themselves with some family of distinction, and, like the butterfly in the sunbeam, to forget the condition from which they had emerged. Some amusing instances of this infirmity are preserved.* In January 1818, Mr John Morgan writes to M. Morgan, Procureur-General at Amiens.† The following are extracts from his letter :—" Permit me to request the favour of you to examine the enclosed armorial bearings, which I presume to do in consequence of the similarity of name. At same time, will you have the goodness to endeavour to obtain an explanation of the inscription on these armorial bearings, which belonged to a General William Morgan, who was in the French service during the years 1745-46." And farther :—" About the month of August last, I had the armorial bearings transmitted to Messrs Vassal & Coy., in Paris, to procure an explanation, as well as to obtain information respecting General William Morgan and Dr William Morgan ; but I have not yet received any satisfactory account of either, which is the cause of my presuming to trouble you." This letter led to no satisfactory result ; and we find Mr Morgan thus addressing Sir William Houston at a subsequent period :—" I have been many years employed on a similar search, and found all the records sadly mutilated from the rebellions in 1715 and 1745, and the parochial registers carelessly kept. My object was to trace back my descent from the Morgans of Glenesk, in Forfarshire, who swore fealty to Edward the First when he overran Scotland in 1296." The thought of connecting himself with his native town by some permanent memorial appears to have been for a season suppressed, but it again from time to time revived. In the year 1830, Mr Morgan transmitted to the Convener of the Nine Incorporated Trades of Dundee a donation of one hundred pounds, to be applied for the benefit of their poor members. The Trades acknowledged, as in duty bound, this handsome gift, and created Mr Morgan an honorary member of their Incorporation. He appears to have been much flattered by the compliment. Baffled in his attempts to identify his family with the French General Morgan, or the

* Appendix No. VIII. † Appendix No. IX.

2

Morgans of Glenesk, another idea now took possession of the mind of John Morgan. He resolved to be the founder of a family which was to throw the Morgans of France, Germany, and Glenesk into the shade. His fortune was to accumulate till it reached the sum of one million sterling, and then it was to be invested in the purchase of lands in the counties of Forfar or the Lothians. The estates were to be strictly entailed. The heir in possession was to assume the name of John Morgan, and Mr Morgan actully selected a gentleman of his acquaintance on whose descendants this golden shower was destined to alight. One cannot help smiling as he reads the document containing these extraordinary provisions. It bears date the 4th January 1836. A change, however, again came over the spirit of his dream. The will to which we have alluded was most carefully obliterated by Mr Morgan, so much so, that it is difficult to decipher its contents; and by a writing subjoined to it he specially annuls all its provisions. The last-mentioned writing, which bears date the 10th October 1842, declares his "wish to establish in the town of Dundee and shire of Forfar an Hospital, strictly in size, the management of the interior of said Hospital in every way as Heriot's Hospital in Edinburgh is conducted." On reflection, he had come to think that his fortune, which had been impaired by losses through the failure of his agents in London and Calcutta, would be inadequate to the building and support of an institution projected on so large a scale as Heriot's Hospital, in Edinburgh; and by a subsequent writing, dated the 20th October 1842, he restricts the Hospital to such a size as shall accommodate only "one hundred boys, in place of one hundred and eighty boys." These two last writings, which are much altered and obliterated, formed the groundwork of the litigation which subsisted for some years, and issued in their being declared, by a judgment of the House of Lords, to constitute a good and valid bequest of the fortune of John Morgan, or so much thereof as shall be sufficient for the purpose of building and endowing an Hospital for the education and maintenance of 100 boys in the town of Dundee. The sum ultimately fixed by the Court, and payable, free of expense, for that purpose, was £73,500. · The history of that litigation is familiar to the inhabitants of this town, and need not be related here. It is instructive, in so far as it shows that the liberality of the friends of education here has succeeded in securing for the town of Dundee the greatest educational boon, so far as money is concerned, which it has yet enjoyed. It has been frequently said that the inhabitants of Dundee were much to blame for not putting forward their claim at an earlier stage of the contention which arose amongst the parties claiming to be the nearest of kin to the late John Morgan, and as such entitled to his fortune. But with that contention the inhabitants of Dundee had truly no concern, and no interest to intermeddle. It may, however, be as well to state that in the course pursued by them they followed the highest professional advice which could be obtained in Scotland. Those who took an active share in superintending the proceedings on behalf of the inhabitants of Dundee acted under the impression that it was due to the memory of Mr Morgan, as well as to the town, to obtain the judgment of the highest tribunal in the land; and the appeal to that tribunal realised all that could have been hoped for by the friends of education amongst us.

Let us not, however, indulge in self-complacency on this account. Let us rather seek to render the munificent bequest of Mr Morgan subservient to the design of its founder and the best interests of those for whom it was intended. The course of instruction to be afforded to the boys admitted into the Hospital comprehends tuition in the English language, literature, and composition, in history and geography, arithmetic, writing, and bookkeeping, besides any other branches which the Governors may from time to time introduce; and the scheme farther provides that religious exercises shall be statedly performed in the house, and that religious instruction shall form a prominent part of the education of the boys. In the choice of a Head-Master the Governors have selected a gentleman whose qualifications have been attested by parties on whose judgment they can place reliance, and who has earned for himself a high reputation as an efficient and successful teacher of youth. Under his charge, we have no doubt that the health and comfort of the boys will be carefully attended to, that their education will be vigorously and successfully carried on, and that it will be the constant aim of the instruction given by him to implant and cherish in the pupils those principles which go to the formation of virtuous and religious character, so that the youths shall find within these walls a comfortable home, whilst they enjoy the advantages of a sound and useful education; and when the time comes for them to leave the Hospital and engage in the duties of active life, they will best evince their sense of gratitude for the benefits conferred upon them here by a course of conduct which shall reflect credit upon themselves and upon the Institution in which they were reared. This will prove at once the most acceptable return to their instructors, and the highest tribute to the memory of John Morgan, their benefactor, and the founder of the Hospital.

SCHEME

ERECTION AND ENDOWMENT OF THE HOSPITAL.

1. Out of the personal estate of the deceased John Morgan, formerly of Coates Crescent, in the city of Edinburgh, the sum of £79,138, 12s. 6d. of the three per cent. Government Annuities which belonged to the deceased, being the exact equivalent at noon on 18th December 1860, of the sum of £73,500 sterling, shall be vested in the following persons, viz. :—

The Provost of Dundee.

The Sheriff of Forfarshire.

One of the Sheriff-Substitutes of Forfarshire, to be named by the Sheriff.

The Dean of Guild of Dundee ; and

The Convener of the Nine Incorporated Trades of Dundee.
All for the time being, as Trustees for the establishment, endowment, and maintenance in all time coming of an Hospital in Dundee, for the education, lodging, boarding, and clothing of 100 Boys, the sons of tradesmen, mechanics, and persons of the working-class generally, whose parents stand in need of assistance to enable them to educate their families, or who are orphans in need of such assistance. Any three of the said Trustees shall be a quorum, and the Hospital shall be known and called by the name of the Morgan Hospital.

2. So much of the said sum as shall not be expended, as hereinafter provided, in acquiring a site for the Hospital, the erection of suitable buildings, and the purchase of all necessary furniture for the same, shall be invested by the said Trustees, under the direction of the Governors of the Hospital, in good and sufficient heritable securities, or in such other securities as the Trustees and Governors may, with the sanction of the Court, in either Division thereof, from time to

time approve and select; and the annual proceeds of all
such investments shall be applied for the purposes of the
Hospital.*

3. All lands, buildings, and other heritages, acquired or
erected for the purposes of the Hospital, shall be vested in
the said Trustees, who shall be bound to pay the expense of
acquiring or erecting the same. And the said Trustees shall
also be at all times bound, when required by the Governors,
to execute all necessary deeds and writings in connection
with the management of the property vested in them, and in
particular all mandates and other writings necessary for the
receipt, by the Treasurer of the Hospital, to be appointed as
hereinafter provided, of the revenues and produce of the said
property.

4. The Governors of the Hospital shall be twenty in number, of whom the six following persons shall be Governors
ex officio:—

The Provost of Dundee.
One of the Sheriff-Substitutes of Forfarshire, to be named
    by the Sheriff.
The Minister of the parish of Dundee.
The Dean of Guild of Dundee.
The Convener of the Nine Incorporated Trades of Dundee.
The Deacon of the Fraternity of Maltmen of Dundee.

And each of the following seven bodies shall elect two
Governors, of whom one shall retire annually, but be eligible
for re-election, viz.:—

The Magistrates and Town Council of Dundee.
The Magistrates and Town Council of Forfar.
The Magistrates and Town Council of Arbroath.
The Magistrates and Town Council of Montrose.
The Presbytery of Dundee.
The Nine Incorporated Trades of Dundee.
The Directors of the High School of Dundee.

In the event of any of the said bodies at any time failing
to make such election within one month of the time which
shall be appointed for their doing so, the Governors shall
elect in their place; and in the event of the death or resig-
nation of an elected Governor, the body by whom he was

* Appendix No. X.

elected, or, on their failure, the remaining Governors, shall be entitled to supply the vacancy.

5. The Governors shall hold not less than four General Meetings in each year, on such days as shall be fixed; and, on a requisition by any three or more Governors, a Special Meeting shall be summoned at any time. At every Meeting any seven of the Governors shall be a quorum; and the Provost of Dundee, or, in his absence, any Governor elected by the Meeting, shall be Chairman, and shall have a casting as well as a deliberative vote.

6. The Governors shall acquire, for the purposes of the Hospital, three acres or thereby of ground, on the lands of Craigie, lying to the east of the town of Dundee, or in such other situation in or near Dundee as the Governors shall consider suitable, and shall cause such ground to be properly enclosed, and a building to be erected thereon, as nearly as conveniently may be, in conformity to a plan prepared by Messrs Peddie & Kinnear, architects in Edinburgh, to which building there shall be attached a Janitor's Lodge; and that portion of the ground not occupied by buildings shall be laid out, partly as play-ground for the Boys, and partly as garden-ground.* And the Governors shall provide for such building, with the exception of the part set aside as a residence for the Head-Master, all necessary furniture, of a good and substantial kind, but plain, and without ornament.

7. The general Management of the Hospital shall be vested in the Governors, who, out of the funds at their disposal, shall maintain the buildings and furniture in good order and repair, and insure the same against fire, and pay all taxes and burdens for which they may be liable, and shall also make such regulations as they may think proper in regard to the dietary and general treatment of the Boys, the duties of the several Masters, the work to be done by the Servants, and the whole internal affairs of the Hospital.

8. The Governors shall nominate and appoint a fit and proper person to be Treasurer and Clerk to the Hospital, to hold office during their pleasure, and shall require the person so nominated and appointed to find security for his intromissions to an extent not exceeding £1000 sterling, and shall

* Appendix No. XI.

pay him, as remuneration for his services, such an annual sum as they may think proper.

9. The Treasurer and Clerk shall call and attend all Meetings of the Governors, keep the minutes of such Meetings, and conduct all correspondence on the affairs of the Hospital. He shall superintend the investment of the funds as hereinbefore provided, draw and receive all the revenues and produce thereof, and pay the same into Bank, to the credit of the Hospital account, in such a manner, and at such times, as never to have in his hands an amount of cash exceeding £10 sterling, under the penalty of being charged with interest on such excess at the rate of 20 per cent. per annum, during the time he shall have retained the same. He shall also make payment of all sums of money, for which he shall receive the authority of a Meeting of the Governors, or of a Committee of their number, duly authorized to grant such authority, and shall discharge such other duties in connection with the Management of the Hospital as the Governors shall direct.

10. The Governors shall, from time to time, fix on one of the Chartered Banks, with which an account shall be kept in name of the Hospital; and the Treasurer shall pay into such account the revenues and produce of the whole property belonging to the Hospital, together with the interest which may accrue thereon; and the said account shall be operated upon, and sums drawn therefrom, by means of cheques or orders signed by the Treasurer and two or more of the Governors, and not otherwise.

11. The account of charge and discharge of the Treasurer's intromissions, together with the vouchers and instructions of the same, shall, once every year, be examined and chequed by an Auditor, to be named for that purpose by the Governors; and such Auditor shall cause abstracts of the said accounts to be prepared and transmitted to the Governors, along with a Report by him, stating whether the income of the Hospital for the year has been exceeded by the expenditure, or the contrary, and specifying the amount of the deficiency or surplus.

12. If at any time it shall appear that the sums paid or payable during any year, for the purposes herein directed, exceed the clear available income and revenue of such year,

such excess shall be re-imbursed and made good out of the first monies which shall be received on account of the Hospital; and the Governors shall thereupon, at their discretion, decrease or alter all or any of the yearly and other payments out of the funds of the Hospital, so, and in such a manner, as that the same shall not exceed the said yearly income and revenue.

13. When, and as often as the Auditor, named as hereinbefore directed, shall report that there remains a surplus of the income and revenue of the Hospital above the annual expenditure, it shall be competent for the Governors to appropriate and apply such surplus in any way which they shall consider most likely to promote the increased efficiency of the Hospital; but any investment of such surplus, other than depositing it in bank, shall be made in name of the Trustees hereinbefore appointed, and in heritable securities, or such other securities, as the Trustees and Governors may, with the sanction of the Court, in either Division thereof, approve and select.

14. The number of Boys to be admitted into the Hospital shall not exceed 100; and their admission shall take place at meetings of the Governors specially called for the purpose: But, during the first year after the building is completed, and ready to be inhabited, not more than 40 Boys shall be admitted; and in like manner, not more than 30 Boys shall be admitted during each of the second and third years respectively, besides supplying any vacancies that may have occurred among those previously admitted.

15. No Boy shall be admitted into the Hospital until he shall have attained the age of 7 years complete, nor after he shall have attained the age of 9 years complete; and no Boy shall be permitted to continue in the Hospital after he shall have attained the age of 14 years complete.

16. In order to the admission of any Boy, it shall be necessary that it be established to the satisfaction of the Governors, that either the father or mother of such Boy is (or, if dead, was) an inhabitant of, and born and educated in one or other of the towns of Dundee, Forfar, Arbroath, or Montrose; but the sons of persons, inhabitants of, and born and educated in Dundee, shall have the preference.

17. The instruction to be afforded shall comprehend the following branches, besides any others which the Governors may from time to time introduce, viz. :—

Religious Instruction.

English Language, Literature, and Composition.

History.

Geography.

Arithmetic.

Writing and Book-keeping.

Vocal Music.

Such boys as discover superior talent shall also be instructed by the Head-Master in one or more of the following branches, viz. :—Latin, Greek, Mathematics, Algebra ; and it shall also be competent for the Governors to direct that such Boys should receive special instruction in any other branches, for which occasional Teachers may be provided.

18. Every Boy beyond the age of 9 years complete, shall, unless specially exempted by the Head-Master, attend for as many hours during each week as the Governors shall direct, a class for instruction in one or other of the trades of a tailor, shoemaker, or carpenter, or such other branch of industrial employment as the Governors shall direct ; and the Governors shall appoint suitable instructors in every such trade or employment, and shall remunerate them in such a manner as they shall think proper ; and it shall be competent to the Governors, on occasion of any Boy leaving the Hospital, to permit such Boy, as a reward for good conduct, to receive the whole or any part of the profits of his work during the preceding year.

19. The Boys shall attend Divine Service, once at least every Sunday, in such place of public worship in connection with the Church of Scotland as the Governors shall appoint, and on every such occasion shall be accompanied by one at least of the Masters. But if the parents or guardians of any Boy shall object to his giving such attendance, it shall be competent for the Governors to make any arrangements that may seem to them proper and suitable, to enable such Boy to attend Divine Service in any other place of worship.

20. The Governors shall elect and appoint a Head-Master, whose duty it shall be to exercise, under their directions, a

general superintendence over all the inmates of the Hospital, and himself to instruct the more advanced Boys. He shall every day conduct, or, in his necessary absence, cause one of the Assistant-Masters to conduct, morning and evening worship in the Chapel, and shall, subject to the approval of the Governors, assign to each of the Assistant-Masters the share which such Master shall take, both in the daily instruction of the Boys, and in superintending them during the preparation of their lessons, and shall perform such other duties appertaining to his office as the Governors may direct. Such Head-Master shall receive an annual salary of not less than £200, besides the use of a free house attached to the Hospital, with coal, gas, and water.

21. The Governors shall elect and appoint two Assistant-Masters, of whom one at least shall always reside in the Hospital, and shall exercise, in the necessary absence of the Head-Master, the general superintendence vested in him. Each of the Assistant-Masters shall be subject to the general directions of the Head-Master, and shall perform such duties in connection with the teaching and superintendence of the Boys as shall be assigned to him by the Head-Master, with the approval of the Governors, and shall receive such annual salary as the Governors shall appoint.

22. It shall be competent for the Governors at any time to dispense with the services of the Head-Master, or of either of the Assistant-Masters, upon giving them six months' notice, or half a year's salary : Provided always, that no resolution to that effect shall be valid, unless it shall have received the approval of a majority of the Governors in office at the time ; and it shall be competent for the Head-Master, or either of the Assistant-Masters, to leave the Hospital, on giving six months' notice, or on forfeiture of half a year's salary, but not otherwise, without special permission from the Governors.

23. For a grave offence, it shall be competent for the Governors to dismiss the Head-Master, or either of the Assistant-Masters, without any such notice or payment of salary as is hereinbefore provided.

24. If at any time the Head-Master, or either of the Assistant-Masters, shall be disqualified by age or permanent infirmity for the continued discharge of his duties, it shall be

competent for the Governors, if there are sufficient funds at their disposal, to award to such Master, in name of retiring allowance, such an annual sum, not exceeding two-thirds of his salary, and under such conditions and limitations as they may think proper.

25. For the instruction of the Boys in Vocal Music and any other branches of education which the Governors shall think fit to introduce, but which it is not possible or advisable should be taught by the permanent Masters, it shall be competent for the Governors to appoint from time to time suitable teachers, who shall visit the Hospital at such hours, and shall receive such remuneration, as the Governors shall direct.

26. All books, papers, pens, pencils, and stationery necessary for the use of the Boys shall be provided by the Governors, who shall also, at their discretion, expend a small sum annually in the purchase of books for a Library, to which the Boys shall have access, under such regulations as the Head-Master, with the approval of the Governors, shall prescribe.

27. It shall be the duty of the Governors, once at least in every year, to provide for the inspection of the Hospital by an educational Inspector of known experience, character, and ability. Such Inspector shall inspect the different classes, by subjecting them to such an examination, either oral or written, or both, as shall, in his opinion, be sufficient to test the efficiency of the teaching, and the progress of the Boys, and shall give in to the Governors a written Report containing the result of his inspection, and any suggestions he may have to offer, as to the improvements in the mode of teaching or otherwise, which Report shall be engrossed for preservation in the Minute-Book of the Governors, and may also, if they shall consider it expedient, be published.

28. The Governors shall appoint a Matron, with a suitable allowance, besides free board and lodging in the Hospital, whose duty it shall be to engage, under their directions, a suitable number of female servants, whom she shall have power to dismiss at her discretion. She shall superintend, in conjunction with the Head-Master, the whole domestic arrangements of the Hospital, receive and be responsible for such provisions and stores of all kinds as may have been contracted for or ordered under the sanction of the Governors;

regulate, under their directions, the dietary of all the inmates; take charge of the Boys' clothes; carefully attend to their health, in which she shall be assisted by one of the female servants as nurse, and shall perform such other duties appertaining to her situation as the Governors may direct.

29. The Governors shall appoint a Warder, with suitable wages, besides free board and lodging in the Hospital, whose duty it shall be to act as Drill-Serjeant, to attend in the Dining-hall and preserve order during meals; to superintend a certain number of the Boys when in their dormitories; and to be with them, when required, in the play-ground, or in their walks. He shall be bound to conform himself in all respects to the orders of the Head-Master, and to render assistance in everything connected with the Hospital, or the Boys, when desired by the Matron.

30. The Governors shall appoint a Janitor, who shall occupy, rent free, the Porter's Lodge, with suitable wages, besides coal and gas, and shall take the charge of keeping a portion of the ground attached to the Hospital in proper cultivation as a Vegetable Garden, in which he shall be assisted by the Boys.

31. The Governors shall provide for the regular visitation of the inmates of the Hospital by a competent medical man, who shall receive such annual remuneration, and perform such duties with reference to the inspection of the Boys, previous to their admission, and otherwise, as the Governors may direct.

32. No one of the Trustees, Governors, Treasurer and Clerk, Head-Master, or Assistant-Masters, shall, either directly or indirectly, enter into any contract in reference to the affairs of the Hospital, or in any manner of way intromit with the Hospital property, otherwise than as is herein provided.

33. The Governors shall have power from time to time to make bye-laws, for the purpose of carrying this scheme into effect, such bye-law not being inconsistent with any of the provisions herein contained; and if at any time it shall appear to a majority of three-fourths of the whole Governors in office at the time, that the objects of the Scheme would be promoted by an alteration of any of the said provisions, it shall be competent for them, with the sanction of the Court of

Session in either Division thereof, obtained on summary application to that effect, to adopt any such alteration: Provided always that no change shall be made in the number or class of Boys for whose benefit the Hospital is intended, or in the preference given to the sons of persons, inhabitants of, and born and educated in Dundee, over the sons of such inhabitants of Forfar, Arbroath, or Montrose.

The above Scheme is authenticated as referred to in the Interlocutor of the Second Division of the Court of Session, of date the 8th day of February 1861, by

JOHN INGLIS, *I.P.D.*

REGULATIONS.

1. It shall be the duty of the Head-Master, under such conditions as may be fixed by the Governors, to watch over the Hospital in all its details, to see that the Teachers are diligent and faithful in the discharge of their duties in their respective Class-Rooms, and otherwise ; and he shall take special care that everything shall be done with propriety, order, and regularity. He shall be exemplary in his own conduct, and see that all others attend faithfully, honestly, and properly to their duties. In case of neglect or disobedience, he shall endeavour to bring the offenders to a sense of their error, so as to prevent a recurrence of the offence ; or otherwise, shall be bound to give information to the Convener of the Committee whose province it is to deal with the matter, until a meeting of such Committee can be held.

2. He shall have power to chastise or otherwise punish the children in a suitable and temperate manner. All offences for which chastisements of importance are inflicted shall be entered in a book kept for that purpose, for the inspection of the Governors.

3. The more degrading kinds of corporal punishment shall be avoided, or resorted to as seldom as possible, and never for mere literary deficiency, if unaccompanied with moral blame. They shall not be inflicted in the private classes, but only in what is called the "Public School," in presence of the Assistant-Masters and the whole of the Boys.

4. While the more ordinary punishments are left for the consideration and sound discretion of the Masters, it is earnestly recommended, that, as far as possible, preventives of faults be employed. Confinement during play-hours, or on Saturday afternoons, and others of a similar kind, may be tried ; but all such shall be entered in the Punishment-Book.

5. Boys shall be subject to punishment for the following

faults in particular, which they are earnestly exhorted to guard against:—

(1). For lying, or for concealment of the truth; for dishonesty; for unbecoming language and behaviour; and any other immorality.

(2). For disrespect and disobedience to those set over them, or in charge of them.

(3). For all disorderly behaviour, whereby the peace and good order of the House may be disturbed.

(4). For rudeness to one another, and for unkind and oppressive treatment of younger Boys.

(5). For disfiguring or destroying any part of the Hospital, Furniture, Shrubs, Plants, or any property belonging to the Hospital.

(6). For wilful idleness, and inattention or indifference to study.

(7). For slovenly habits, and want of punctuality.

(8). For quitting the precincts of the Hospital without permission.

(9). On frequently repeated instances of any of the above faults, or on individual cases of a more aggravated nature, the Head-Master shall immediately report to the House Committee, that they and the General Board may deal with the matter as they shall see fit, either by depriving the delinquent of some of his privileges, or by expelling him from the Hospital.

(10). As a constant warning to the Boys, the preceding Regulations shall be printed and hung up in each of the Class-rooms and Wards, and a copy exhibited to the Parents or Guardians of the Boys on their admission into the Hospital.

6. The Boys shall attend Divine Service once at least every Sabbath, in such place of public worship, in connection with the Church of Scotland, as the Governors shall appoint; and on every such occasion they shall be accompanied by one of the Masters: But if the Parents or Guardians of any Boy shall object to his giving such attendance, it shall be competent for the Governors to make such arrangements as seem proper and suitable to enable the Boy to attend Divine Service in any other place of worship. When it is found at any

time necessary, from any cause, that the whole or any considerable number of the Boys shall be kept at home instead of going to Church, one of the Masters shall remain with them and give them religious instruction.

7. The Head-Master shall every day perform, or, in his necessary absence, cause one of the Assistant-Masters to perform, Morning and Evening Devotions in the Chapel, at the hour to be ordered by the Governors, and shall see that all the Children, and every other person within the Hospital, regularly attend, unless for reasons satisfactory to him.

8. The superintendence of the religious and moral training of the Boys shall devolve upon the Head-Master, as the responsible head of the Institution. It shall accordingly be his duty to give, or see that the Assistant-Masters give, daily, the requisite instruction in the Bible and Shorter Catechism; and in addition to this, he shall, as often as he deems it expedient—but regularly on the Sabbath evenings—convene them all in the Chapel, and give them such religious instruction, in the way of address, exposition, exercises, or otherwise, as may tend to encourage them in the cultivation of piety, to imbue their minds with correct views of Divine truth, and to form them to those dispositions and habits upon which their well-being and happiness throughout life so essentially depend.

9. He shall report half-yearly, or as often as may be required, to the Education Committee, on the number and state of the different classes, and any other matters relating to them that require to be attended to; it being understood, that, if anything of importance shall occur at any time, he shall immediately submit a report on the subject to the Education Committee; and, with a view to making his report, he shall daily visit the different Class-Rooms, to see that the Teachers are diligent in their duties, and the Boys orderly, cleanly, well-behaved, and attentive.

10. He shall be present every day when the Boys are at their meals, or as frequently as he finds convenient, consistently with the discharge of his other duties; and he shall take care that the Warder, and at least one of the Assistant-Masters, according to his instructions, are present at each of the Boys' meals, and see that everything is done with

3

decency, cleanliness, and order; and a Grace before and Thanksgiving after each meal shall be audibly pronounced, either by himself or one of the Assistant-Masters by his appointment.

11. He, with one of the Assistant-Teachers and the Warder, shall, every morning, when the Boys are first convened, either in their School-Room or Dining-Hall, see that they are all neat and clean in their dress and person; and in like manner, he shall, every night, when the Boys are going to bed, visit the Dormitories, and see that the Boys are all present, and that everything necessary is provided and in proper order for them, and that they go regularly to bed, after performing their private Devotions; also, that they fold or put up their Clothes as shall be directed; or he shall take care that this duty is performed by at least one of the Teachers and Warder, according to his instructions.

12. He shall take care that all the Outer Doors of the Building are locked at eight o'clock P.M. during the summer months, and at half-past seven o'clock P.M. during the winter months, and the keys of all the doors, except the door of the Principal Entrance, shall at that hour be lodged with him, or, in his absence, with one of the Teachers, as may be directed by him. The key of the Main Entrance-Door shall be left in a place to be appointed for that purpose, till ten o'clock P.M.; after which hour no stranger shall be allowed to remain in the Hospital; and at that hour the key of the Entrance-Door shall be brought to his room. Eleven o'clock P.M. shall be the latest hour at which any of the Inmates shall be out of the House. All exceptional cases, which shall be allowed only on leave being specially asked and obtained from the Head-Master, shall be entered by him in his reports to the House Committee.

13. He shall at all times, when required, give every aid and assistance in his power to the Medical Attendant of the Hospital; and it shall be his duty, along with the Matron, to take care that the orders of the Medical Attendant are faithfully attended to, and that everything necessary and proper be done, in order to contribute to the recovery and comfort of such of the Boys as may be prevented from attending School or Church, in consequence of bad health.

14. He shall, with the assistance of the Warder, have the charge of the Wardrobe of the Boys (except the Linens and Stockings), and shall examine their Clothes, and see that they are in terms of the Rules of the Hospital, and in good order. He shall also take the superintendence of the whole Buildings, and everything else within the bounds of the Hospital, and communicate with the House Committee or Treasurer, when necessary, giving immediate notice of any repairs that may be needed.

15. He shall keep a set of Account-Books, according to instructions to be given by the Treasurer, in which shall be entered all orders to be given for Provisions, Stores, Clothing, and others, as may have been contracted for, or ordered under the sanction of the Governors; and also daily, or as often as necessary, inspect the Matron's Accounts or Memorandum-Books of what Provisions or others may be handed over to her for the use of the Hospital; and these shall at all times be open for the inspection of the House Committee, Treasurer, or Auditor to the Hospital; and all instructions to be given from time to time regarding the mode of keeping such Books and Accounts shall be faithfully attended to; and he shall satisfy himself that the receipts and disbursements of Provisions, &c., committed to his charge are all correct. He shall examine and check the Monthly or Weekly Bills, and shall attest all Accounts of Supplies received for the Hospital as correct, before they are presented to the Treasurer for payment; and when any Provisions or other Stores are brought to the Hospital, and reported to him by the Matron or others having charge thereof to be inferior in quality, or deficient in weight, he shall, without loss of time, inform the Convener of the House Committee, or the Treasurer thereof, and shall include this circumstance in his next report to the House Committee. He shall prepare an Inventory of the whole apparatus of the School-Rooms, which he shall submit annually to the Education Committee, and shall likewise keep an accurate account of the Boys' Clothing, and of all other Supplies placed under his charge, together with a statement of the Cast-Clothing, for distribution, according to the directions of the Governors.

16. He shall keep a copy of the Inventory of the Cooking

Utensils, &c. &c., intrusted to the charge of the Matron, and he shall compare these Articles with the Inventory at least once a year, or oftener, when it may appear to him to be necessary.

17. He shall regularly submit his own Report Books to all the Meetings of the Education and House Committees, but more particularly to the Meetings held immediately before the General Meetings of the Governors, at which any reports or suggestions in them require to be considered.

18. When Boys are about to attain the fourteenth year of their age, he shall, by letter, communicate to the relatives, one month at least before their attaining that age, so that they may not be taken unawares in their having to leave the Hospital. He shall not accept of any gratuity whatever from any relation or friend of any of the Boys, or from any person who may be employed or contracted with to supply any Articles for the use of the Hospital, on pain of immediate dismissal; nor shall he permit any such gratuity to be received, with his knowledge, by any other person employed in the Establishment; and, in case of his detecting anything of the kind, he shall give instant information to the Convener of the House Committee.

19. He shall never be a night absent without special leave given to him by the Convener, or, in his absence, by some other member of the House Committee.

20. If he shall at any time be under any difficulty with regard to the application of these Regulations, or if any case shall occur which is not provided for in them, he shall act in the exercise of a sound discretion as he thinks best, after consulting with the Convener, or, in his absence, with any other member of the Committee whose province it is to deal with the matter, until a Meeting of such Committee can be held and consulted.

NOTE.—The age of the Head-Master not to be under twenty-five nor above forty years at the time of his appointment ; and this condition not to be departed from without the consent of three-fourths of the Governors.

II.—THE MATRON.

The Matron shall hold her appointment during the pleasure of the Governors. On her appointment, and before taking her charge, she shall be furnished with a copy of the Rules and Regulations, which, as well as such other instructions as she may receive from the Governors from time to time, she shall be bound to observe in all respects.

1. She shall have the general superintendence, under the Head-Master, of the whole Establishment; for the cleanliness and good order of which, so far as placed under her, and the charge of the Female Officials and Servants, she shall be held responsible. As head of the Female part of the Establishment, she shall have special authority over all the Female Officials, who shall obey her in the performance of their duties. In case of neglect or disobedience on the part of any of them, she shall endeavour to bring the offenders to a sense of their error; or otherwise, she shall give information thereof to the Head-Master, who, in presence of the Matron, shall admonish the person complained of; and if these admonitions shall not have the effect of preventing a recurrence of the offence, he shall give information to the Convener, or, in his absence, to any other member of the House Committee. She shall be regular and exemplary in her own conduct, and take particular care that all the Female Servants attend faithfully, honestly, and properly to their duties.

2. She shall attend at the Daily Morning and Evening Devotions. She shall regulate with propriety the Diet of the Assistant-Master and Warder who reside in the Hospital, and attend carefully to the Dietary of the Boys, as that may from time to time be agreed on and fixed by the House Committee; and she shall see that all the victuals required for the Establishment are cleanly and properly cooked and served out, and that the Dining-rooms are regularly swept and cleaned.

3. She shall, on any case of sickness occurring, immediately send notice to the Medical Attendant, and shall at the same time inform the Head-Master; and she shall at all times give every aid and assistance in her power to the Medical Attendant, and shall take care that all victuals and medicine ordered by him for the Boys shall be duly and regularly given and administered; and it shall be her special duty to take care that everything necessary and proper be done by the Nurses and others in charge of the Sick or Invalid Children, in order

to contribute to their recovery, and to the comfort of such of the Boys as may be prevented from attending School, or from attending Church, in consequence of bad health. She shall at all times have a careful eye to the state of health of the Boys, with the view of discovering whether any of them are delicate or labouring under any complaints of which they themselves may have made no mention.

4. She shall have charge of the Wardrobe of all the Children in the House, with the exception of the Boys' Outer Clothes, Caps, and Shoes; shall examine, when received into the House, the articles committed to her charge, and see that they are proper, and as ordered by the Governors. She shall also have charge and keep an Inventory of all the Linen, Blankets, &c. She shall annually, at a stated period, draw out an Inventory of all such articles, which she shall enter in a book to be kept for the purpose, and of which a copy shall be given to the Treasurer. She shall have charge of the Stores of Tea, Sugar, &c., and shall make regular and immediate entries in a book kept for that purpose of every article of Stores delivered to her, and how the same shall have been disposed of; and she shall give immediate notice to the Head-Master or to the Treasurer, should any part of the articles above mentioned sent to her charge be inferior in quality or deficient in quantity.

5. She shall have the charge of all the Furniture and Utensils within the House. An Inventory of the whole shall be taken at the commencement of her charge, and one copy thereof shall be engrossed in a book to be kept by the Head-Master at the Hospital for the inspection of the Governors, and another copy shall be given to the Matron; and from time to time every other article of Furniture and Utensil provided and coming under her charge shall be added to both copies of the Inventory; and these articles shall be examined and compared by her with the Inventories at each term of Whitsunday, and all the variations marked in the Inventories and reported to the Treasurer. It shall be her duty to see that the whole of the Furniture, and also the Apartments in the House, shall be kept clean and in good order. She shall also have the whole charge of the Family Linens, Body Linen, Underclothing, and Stockings of the Boys, and shall

examine them when received into the House, and see they are in terms of the Regulations of the Hospital, and in good order; and particular Inventories thereof shall be kept by her for the inspection of the Governors.

6. She shall keep a regular and distinct account of such sums of money as may from time to time be paid to her by the Treasurer, for the purpose of defraying any immediate and incidental expenses not otherwise provided for, and also of the expenditure of such sums; which accounts she shall deliver at least once a month to the Treasurer, to be examined by him before being engrossed in the general accounts.

7. She shall have the power of selecting and engaging the Female Servants, and of removing them from their situations, according to the best of her judgment; using every means in her power to procure and retain the services of proper persons, and she shall advise with the Head-Master before dismissing them.

8. She shall not permit the Female Servants to leave the Hospital, except at such times as she may deem convenient and proper, and on no account suffer any of them to be absent after the hour appointed for the Family Devotions at night, without the special permission of the Head-Master; nor shall she allow them to receive any Vistors in the Hospital without her leave.

9. She shall never be a night absent without special leave given to her by the Convener of the House Committee.

10. She shall not be allowed to accept of any gratuity from any relation or friend of any of the Boys, or from any person who may be employed or contracted with to supply any articles for the use of the Hospital, on pain of immediate dismissal; nor shall she premit any such gratuity, with her knowledge, to be received by any other person employed in the Establishment; and in case of her detecting any such, she shall give instant information to the Convener of the House Committee.

11. She shall keep Books and Accounts in the form to be appointed by the Treasurer, and give strict attention to any Bye-Laws or Regulations which may be furnished to her for her guidance, and also attend to the instructions to be given her by the House Committee, and generally to conduct her

whole duties in such a way as to receive the esteem and respect of those under her charge and promote the best interest of the Hospital.

> · NOTE.—The age of the Matron not to be under twenty-five nor above forty years at the time of her appointment; and this condition not to be departed from without the consent of three-fourths of the Governors.

III.—ASSISTANT-MASTERS.

Their duties, so far as not provided for under the General Regulations, shall be defined and pointed out by Regulations prepared by the Head-Master and sanctioned by the House Committee, and which shall be attended to in every respect. They shall make it their special study to promote the education, comfort, and happiness of the Boys under their charge, by gaining their esteem and affection, and shall endeavour to promote the prosperity and efficiency of the Hospital in every respect.

IV.—TREASURER AND CLERK'S DUTIES.

These are defined in the scheme for the Hospital, and he shall attend generally to such duties as may from time to time be fixed by the Governors; and in particular, he shall arrange, as far as possible, the business coming before the Meetings of the Governors and their Commitees. He shall engross the minutes in a book or books to be kept for the purpose. He shall prepare copies of and excerpts from the minutes, when directed to do so, and take charge of the printing of reports and documents which may be directed to be printed. He shall engross, in a record-book, all deeds executed by the Trustees or Governors of the Hospital. He shall issue forms of petitions for the admission of Boys, and conduct all correspondence relative to the admission or removal of the Boys. He shall check the accounts given in to him for payment, and see that all accounts for furnishings to the Hospital are regularly certified by the Head-Master. He shall keep a set of books, containing a distinct account of his intromissions, and a proper record of the pecuniary transactions of the Governors and Trustees, which shall be regularly posted in the different accounts kept in a ledger for the purpose, and he shall take charge of all documents, accounts, and vouchers, or otherwise dispose of them as the Governors shall direct. He shall, under the directions of the Governors, take the necessary steps for procuring tenders and framing contracts for provisions, coals, furnishings, &c. He shall make payment of all salaries, wages, and accounts of the officials and others, as authorized by the Governors.

V.—MEDICAL ATTENDANT.

1. He shall visit the Hospital at least once every week; and in case of the indisposition of any of the inmates, he shall attend immediately on getting intimation thereof, and afterwards as often as may be necessary. At his periodical and other visits, he shall make such observations, with regard not only to the state of the Sick and Invalid Children, but also to the state of health of the Children generally, as may enable him in his Reports to make the Governors acquainted with the general state of health of the whole inmates; and he shall make a report on this subject at least once every six months.

2. It shall be his duty carefully to examine Boys before their admission into the Hospital, and to see that the answers to the different questions contained in a schedule thereof, to be furnished to him, are truthfully given by the Boys, their Parents, or Guardians, at examination, and how far these accord with his own opinion, judging from the appearance of the Boys, and other circumstances which fall under his personal observation.

3. He shall consider and advise the House Committee as to the best mode of procuring medicines for the Inmates of the Hospital, and shall follow out the instructions of the Committee as regards the same.

4. All the Reports made by the Medical Attendant shall be engrossed in a book to be kept for the purpose, which shall be laid on the table at all Meetings of the House Committee and of the Governors, if required.

5. The visitation of the Sick and Convalescent Children by their relations, when such visitation is deemed safe and prudent by the Medical Attendant, shall be under such regula-

tions as he shall consider necessary. The relatives shall be admitted to the Sick Rooms by cards of admission signed by the Medical Attendant, and given to the relatives through the medium of the Matron.

VI.—WARDER'S DUTIES.

These shall be defined by the Head-Master, with the sanction of the House Committee, and shall be strictly attended to.

VII.—JANITOR'S DUTIES.

He shall attend to keeping the Grounds in order, and, with the assistance of such of the Boys as are capable, shall keep a Vegetable Garden for the use of the Hospital. He shall act as Gatekeeper, and keep the Lodge, Offices, Area, and Grounds in a neat and tradesman-like manner, and generally attend to the interests of the Establishment, and to his duties, as these may from time to time be laid down or pointed out to him by the House Committee or Head-Master, making himself generally useful in the Establishment. A Letter-Box shall be provided for the receipt of letters and packages addressed to any inmates of the Hospital, and these shall be delivered by the Janitor immediately on receipt of them.

VIII.—The whole Regulations and Duties of the Officials may be altered, varied, or amended by the Governors, or the Committees intrusted with such, at pleasure ; and the Officials shall be bound to give effect thereto in every respect.

APPENDIX.

No. I.

TESTAMENTARY WRITINGS OF THE LATE JOHN MORGAN, ESQ.,
17 COATES CRESCENT, EDINBURGH, RELATING TO THE HOSPITAL.

NOTE.—*The words in Italics and between Brackets are deleted in the
original documents.*

WRITING No. I.

I, John Morgan, of Edinburgh, do by these presents bequeath to
my sister, Agnes Morgan, the life-rent of all my property, whether
real or personal. I beg and request the favour of the Honble.
Court of Session to nominate a Judicial Factor for the management
of my property, whether real or personal, that is, by laying out this
[*personal property in heritable Bonds on Lands in Scotland until the lands I*]
intend [*purchasing myself, and the amount of the heritable Bonds accumulate to one million of pounds sterling.*] When the [*property has accu-
mulated to one million of pounds sterling, the Judicial Factor will purchase
Lands in the Shires of Forfar*], East and [*Mid Lothians.*] These [*lands
are to be strictly and rigidly entailed according to the laws of*] Scotland
and that no part or portion of these [*lands shall be sold or mortgages
by the life-renter*] who [*may be in possession of the said lands ; also every
one who succeeds to the estate or estates is*] to take [*the name of John
Morgan.*] * * *

I have farther to request of my said sister, Agnes Morgan, and
those who may succeed to this property, to keep in good and sufficient
repairs my brother's tomb in the Greyfriar's Churchyard of Edinburgh, and also my [*father's*] tomb in the burial place of Dundee, when
the tablets are any ways effaced, to renew the inscriptions on both of
these tombs. * * *

My sister, Agnes Morgan, is to have all my silver and plated
ware, wines, coaches, horses, and harness, with jewels of every kind,
as her own property, and that she may dispose of them as she may
think proper. Witness my hand, at Edinburgh, the fourth day of
January one thousand eight hundred and thirty-six years (1836).

(Signed)   JNO. MORGAN.

The Judicial Factor is not to take place until the death of my said
sister, Agnes Morgan. Witness my hand, at Edinburgh, the fourth
day of January, one thousand eight hundred and thirty-six years
(1836).

(Signed)   JNO. MORGAN.

Writing No. II.

Written on a separate leaf, but apparently a part of the same sheet of paper, and a continuation of No. I.

[*George Morgan, who married B. Cramond, can only inherit this property by being the representative of the Cramonds, but not for the name of Morgan even should he be nearest heir male to my said father. Witness my hand, at Edinburgh, the eighteenth day of November one thousand eight hundred and forty years* (1840).

(Signed)   Jno. Morgan.]

Edinburgh, 10*th October* 1842.—I hereby annul all hitherto written on the first, second, and third pages of this, and wish to establish in the town of Dundee, in the shire of Forfar, an [*an Hospital strictly in size, the management of the interior of said Hospital in every way as Heriot's Hospital in Edinburgh is conducted*], the inhabitants born and educated in Dundee to have the preference of the towns of Forfar, Arbroath, and Montrose, but inhabitants of any other county or town are excluded.

(Signed)   Jno. Morgan.

[*The Judicial Factor is not to take place until the death of my sister, Agnes Morgan, and that she is to enjoy during her life the life-rent of all my property, real and personal. Witness my hand, at Edinburgh, the tenth day of October one thousand eight hundred and forty-two years.*

(Signed)   Jno. Morgan.]

I hereby wish only one hundred boys to be admitted in the Hospital at Dundee [*and the structure of the house to be less than that of Heriot's Hospital*], and to contain one hundred boys in place of one hundred and eighty boys.

(Signed)   Jno. Morgan.

Edinburgh, 20*th Oct.* 1842.

Writing No. III.

Note.—*This paper is in the handwriting of* Miss Morgan, *the sister of* Mr Morgan.

John Morgan, 17 Coates Crescent, Edinburgh, 6th September 1846. Do by this bequeath to my sister, Agnes Morgan, the life-rent of all my property, whether real or personal. My sister, Agnes Morgan, is to have all my silver plate, likewise all my furniture, coach, horses, harness, with jewels of every kind, as her own property, and that she may dispose of them as she may think proper. Witness my hand. I beg and request the Honble. Court of Session to nominate a Judicial Factor for the management of my property, whether real or personal, that is, by laying it out to the best advantage after my death, and my sister, Agnes Morgan, to accumulate, for ten years, to erect an Hospital in Dundee to educate the poor children of the Nine Trades, the name of Morgan to be preferred, although they do not belong to Dundee. I wish that the Hospital may not be very expensive, as it is for poor children. The Judicial Factor is not to take place until the death of my sister, Agnes Morgan. If my sister's death was to take place before mine, I wish at my death my house in 17 Coates Crescent, and furniture, to be sold, likewise my house and grounds in Calcutta, the money to go to the fund for the Hospital in Dundee to educate the poor children of the Nine Trades of Dundee, the name of Morgan to be preferred. * * *

(Signed)   JNO. MORGAN.

6th Sept. 1846.

No. II.

MEMORIAL FOR THE MAGISTRATES AND TOWN COUNCIL OF THE ROYAL BURGH OF DUNDEE.

Along with this the Memorialists lay before Counsel a case submitted to John Marshall. Esq., by Messrs Hope, Oliphant, & Mackay, W.S., Agents for the late John Morgan, Esq., and the opinion of Mr Marshall, thereon.

That case contains copies of the various Testamentary Writings by the late Mr Morgan, and explanations of the circumstances connected with them.

No doubt, the Memorialists apprehend, can be entertained that it was the well-considered and fixed resolution of Mr Morgan—a resolution approved of and concurred in by his sister, Miss Morgan— to devote his fortune for the purposes of education in Dundee, his native town. His father, Mr Thomas Morgan, was a brewer in Dundee. John and Thomas Morgan, the sons, went to India and there realized a large fortune. They returned to Scotland about 35 years ago, and lived for a short time at Balgay, in the vicinity of Dundee, whence they removed to Edinburgh. Thomas died about 35 years ago. His brother John succeeded under will to his property. Miss Morgan died in the beginning of the year 1848, and John, the last of the family, died on the 25th of August last.

Various parties have pretended to claim propinquity to Mr Morgan; but up to this period it is believed that no one has been able to adduce legal evidence of relationship to him. It is understood that Mr Donald Lindsay, who was appointed Judicial Factor on the estate of Mr Morgan, proposes to institute an action of Multiplepoinding in the Court of Session, with a view to have the claims of parties discussed and ascertained. The Memorialists, on behalf of the town and community of Dundee, feel deeply interested in the issue of such an action. It is proper to state that they do not set up any claim to the residue of Mr Morgan's estate as in opposition to the claim of the Nine Incorporated Trades, for the education of whose children Mr Morgan seems to have been desirous to make provision; but whatever may be the special destination of the fund, they conceive that it was clearly the intention of Mr Morgan that it should be devoted to the purposes of education in Dundee; and the Memorialists conceive that they are called upon to do what they can to cause that intention to be carried into effect.

The opinion of Counsel is desired in answer to the following queries, which are respectfully submitted for their consideration :—

QUERIES.

1. Taking the various Testamentary Writings together, and looking specially to the holograph writings, dated 10th and 20th October 1842, are they effectual to convey the personal estate of Mr Morgan, or to establish in the Memorialists a title to the said estate, or any portion of it, for the erection and endowment of an Hospital for the purposes of education in Dundee; or does it confer upon the Memorialists a right to insist upon the application of the estate, or any portion of it, to the purposes aforesaid? Or what is the nature and extent of their interest in the estate and succession of the deceased?

2. In judging of the effect of the deletings in the holograph writings referred to, seeing the words "an hospital" are necessary to the sense of the writing dated 10th October 1842, and that this is shewn by the writing dated 20th October 1842, do these writings, taken together, constitute a good and valid Testament, or do the deletings, in the opinion of Counsel, vitiate these writings *in essentialibus*, or to what extent, if any, do they affect the validity of the said writings?

3. Supposing that the Judicial Factor shall raise an action of Multiplepoinding, will the Memorialists be entitled to make appearance in that action, or what steps should they take with a view to obtain a judicial consideration of the claims of the Town and Community of Dundee?

4. To preserve entire the rights of the Memorialists and of the community of Dundee, is it the duty of the Memorialists to certiorate the Judicial Factor of the nature and extent of their claims, and make a demand upon him in respect of their interest in the estate under the Testamentary Writings already referred to?

5. Supposing Counsel shall be of opinion that in virtue of the holograph writings dated 10th October 1842 and 20th October 1842, the Memorialists are entitled to call upon the Judicial Factor to lay aside a sum sufficient to build an Hospital and provide an endowment adequate to the education and maintenance of 100 boys therein, in a manner similar to that in which the boys are maintained and educated in Heriot's Hospital, what steps besides those already suggested should the Memorialists take in furtherance of that object?

6. Supposing the parties who claim relationship to Mr Morgan

shall fail in establishing their claim to the satisfaction of the Court, how will their failure affect the rights of the Memorialists? Again, supposing that the Memorialists do not succeed in establishing a legal title to Mr Morgan's estate, and assuming that it should devolve upon the Crown as *ultima hæres*, would not their equitable title form the ground of an application to the Crown for a gift of the estate, which, according to the usage in similar cases, would probably be successful?

7. Generally, what steps ought the Memorialists to adopt with a view to preserve entire their own rights and the rights of the community of Dundee in the estate of Mr Morgan?

Counsel are requested to state anything which may occur to them in connection with the subject of the Memorial, and the duty of the Memorialists in reference to it.

DUNDEE, *December* 1850.

OPINION FOR THE MAGISTRATES OF DUNDEE.

The questions that arise as to the validity and effect of the writings left by Mr Morgan as regards the Town of Dundee are attended with difficulty.

But we are of opinion that it is the duty of the Memorialists to watch over the competition that is now likely to take place as to the general or residuary interest in Mr Morgan's succession, and to take the proper time for putting forward a claim under the bequest referred to before the fund is divided or otherwise disposed of.

The opinion of

            (Signed)   DUN. M'NEILL.
                  "   CHARLES NEAVES.

EDINBURGH, 12*th Dec.* 1850.

No. III.

REPORT OF A PUBLIC MEETING HELD ON THE 17TH OCTOBER 1855.

A large and influential meeting was held in the Town Hall, Dundee, on Wednesday, the 17th October 1855, called by a circular, in which the Provost and the Convener of the Nine Trades requested the attendance of gentlemen interested in the cause of education in Dundee to hear a communication on the subject of Morgan's Bequest, and the steps which it may be proper to take for the purpose of securing for this town the benefits intended by the testator. Besides a number of our leading townsmen, the meeting was attended by George Duncan, Esq., the Burgh Member, and by Lord Kinnaird. On the motion of Mr Duncan, the Provost was called to the chair.

The Chairman having mentioned the interest which Mr P. H. Thoms had long taken in this matter, requested that gentlemen to state the circumstances under which the meeting had been called.

Mr Thoms, after mentioning how he had been led to take an active interest in this case, proceeded to give an account of Mr Morgan's family. His father, Thomas Morgan, was a brewer in Dundee. The two sons, John and Thomas Morgan, went to India at an early period of their lives, and having there amassed a large fortune, returned upwards of forty years ago to their native country. They left behind them in Dundee two sisters, Matilda and Agnes, who, on their return, lived in family with them at Balgay for some years, and subsequently in Edinburgh, whither they removed, and where they spent the remainder of their lives. Thomas and Matilda died first. Agnes, who was considerably younger than her brother John, died about the beginning of the year 1848, and John Morgan died on the 28th of August 1850, being about ninety years of age. In 1848, his faculties having become impaired by the infirmities of age, it was found necessary to apply to the Court of Session for the appointment of a *curator bonis*, and Mr Lindsay, accountant, was nominated to that office. Mr Morgan, in the year 1830, sent a donation of £100 to be divided amongst the poor of the Nine Incorporated Trades. In acknowledgment of this he was created an honorary member of the Trades, and he wrote a letter (which Mr Thoms read) expressing his high sense of-the compliment, and his deep interest in the welfare of the Trades. Mr Thoms now came to the testamentary deeds, of which a *fac simile* was produced. He went over the deeds to show not only that Mr Morgan had formed the intention of establishing an Hospital for the education of boys in Dundee, but how fixed was his purpose, and how earnest he was that it should be carried into effect. He stated that the deeds had to a certain extent been recognized by the Courts, for the legacies to private individuals had been paid ; and, considering that testamentary writings are of all others most favoured by the law, he had a strong conviction that these writings in the present case formed a good and valid settlement. In reference to the legal bearing of the case, however, he referred to his friend, Mr Dodds, now present. It was proper to state that, having had much intercourse with Mr Dodds, he had naturally been led to converse with him on this subject. They had discussed and debated it together. They had corresponded about it, and latterly Mr Dodds had made an elaborate investigation of the authorities, which led him to the conclusion that the writings left by Mr Morgan made up a good and sufficient will. It was proper to state that in the year 1850 the Nine Trades and the Town Council had taken the advice of eminent Counsel as to the validity of Mr Morgan's settlement. Mr Thoms read the opinion obtained by the Town Council, which was to the effect that they ought to watch the competition which would take place, and at the proper time put forth their claim to the succession. He held that the " proper time " had now arrived, and it was for the community either to take the requisite steps for vindicating their claim or to abandon it altogether. After hearing the statement of Mr Dodds, he was confident that the authorities and inhabitants of Dundee would not willingly give up their claim to a property destined by the testator to the purpose of education in this place, and which, if rightly administered, might confer benefits of the greatest value upon the rising generation amongst us. There was an indication in one of the deeds that the children of the members of the Nine Trades should have a preference over others ; but he regarded the question as one of general importance, and he hoped that all who felt an interest in the cause of education would unite heartily in endeavouring to secure a boon of so much importance to the community at large.

Mr Dodds said he felt great diffidence in rising to address the meeting, not only because he was a stranger to most of the gentlemen present, but because it might excite surprise why he, a stranger, should appear there and address them on a matter which more peculiarly concerned the town of Dundee. Mr Thoms had done him the favour to mention that, some years ago, when engaged together in other business of the town, this Morgan bequest became a subject of accidental conversation between them, and, both from its curiosity and great interest, he had since devoted a good deal of attention to it. Having occasion to be in Dundee at this time, it was thought by several gentlemen that this was a fitting opportunity to hold a meeting to consider whether the town should adopt any steps regarding this bequest ; and he had been requested to attend to aid the object of the meeting by stating generally the views which had occurred to him in his examination of the subject. And it was in compliance with this request that he now stood before them. After the narrative which had been given by Mr Thoms, he was happy to think that the observations which he would require to make would be few, and confined only to the principal legal bearings of the question. He would not trouble the meeting with professional details, or minute legal discussions ; he would keep his observations general ; but he wished it to be understood that he had carefully noted the authorities on which he spoke, and he should make no statement for which he did not feel that he had good authority in law. Leaving all other facts concerning the Morgan family, he should take up the matter as it stood in 1848. At the beginning of that year Miss Morgan died ; and as she had not simply lived in the family with Mr Morgan, and was his sole surviving relative, but had been the active manager of his affairs, his agents thought it right, immediately upon her death, to apply to the Court, and they obtained the appointment (in March or April 1848) of a *curator bonis* to take charge of his estate and interests. This Miss Morgan died in 1848, and in the same year Mr Morgan became civilly dead. The repositories of both were then opened, and the testamentary writings were found upon which the claim of Dundee is based. Some of these were found in the reposi-

4

tories of Miss Morgan; but those to which the real importance attaches were found in those of Mr Morgan, carefully locked up in his writing desk. They were in a state of secure preservation, all connected together, and, under the whole circumstances, would be viewed in law as being found in the repositories of the testator and carefully left by him as his will. Those writings were all holograph of Mr Morgan, except the last in date, which was in the handwriting of Miss Morgan, but signed by Mr Morgan. Let us now briefly examine them, so far at least as they relate to the claim of Dundee. In doing so, we must bear in mind two well-established principles of law in the matter of testaments of personal property, which will direct and simplify our examination of the writings. The first principle is, that where a party leaves a number of documents all of a testamentary character, they must not be taken simply and separately, but must be all laid together, and, viewed as a whole, the light arising from one to be reflected upon the rest, and anything doubtful in one to be supplied by what is clear in the others, so that, from a consideration of the whole, the will or testamentary purpose of the party may be discovered and ascertained. The second principle is, that in testamentary writings, at least in holograph testaments, the mind and intention of the testator is everything, the manner and form are nothing, if only the real intention appear. Under the guidance of those two principles look at the testamentary writings left by Mr Morgan. Copies of those writings are now in the hands of many gentlemen, and may easily be had. In the writings of 10th and 20th October 1842, as they originally stood before any erasure, he distinctly willed his property to be applied to the establishment of an Hospital in Dundee for the education and upbringing of boys of that town, on a similar plan with Heriot's Hospital in Edinburgh. On after reflection—either having taken a prepossession against Heriot's Hospital, or thinking the funds might not be sufficient to rival that vast establishment —he resolved to strike out from the writings all that related to Heriot's Hospital. In the writing of 20th October, he makes the erasure with perfect accuracy; but in the prior writing of 10th October, this old man, now upwards of eighty, in expunging all words relating to Heriot's Hospital, also deletes the two words, "an hospital," which referred to his intended establishment in Dundee, and not to Heriot's, as he evidently supposed. No one, looking into these writings, can doubt that this is the history of the erasure in the document of 10th October. It is manifestly nothing more than a clerical error—a slip of the old man's pen—and it would be so treated in any Court of law. But, suppose this erasure were held to create an essential blank in the writing of 10th October, taken by itself, yet, according to the principle already explained, the writing is not to be taken by itself, but must be taken in connection with the writing of 20th October, which, in the eye of the law, is but one and the same continuous will. And in this writing the "Hospital of Dundee" is expressly specified and defined, thus casting a reflex light over the other writings, which thus constitute together a clear and undoubted testament. Let those two writings be read over together to the gentlemen in this room—(Mr Dodds here read the document)—and could any one say that there was the shadow of a doubt as to the intention of Mr Morgan? Was it not the clear purpose of his mind, the cherished wish of his heart, to devote his property to the establishment of a great Hospital in Dundee? And in the case of wills, especially of holograph wills, clear intention would override every smaller consideration, and any little trifling defect of form. Many examples of this occur both in the law of England and Scotland—which, on the matter of testaments, are nearly the same—and the Courts in both countries are daily becoming more favourable to carry out the intentions of the testator, whatever mere formal defects there may be. (Mr Dodds here quoted a number of cases in illustration). Then, again, in the testamentary writing of 16th June 1843—many months after those previous writings—Mr Morgan bequeaths to Lord Fullerton a legacy of £200, hoping that his Lordship would give advice, if necessary, " respecting my settlement." That is, the settlement in favour of the Hospital in Dundee. It was his firm purpose and belief that he had made a perfect settlement. It so happens, also, that Miss Morgan, in a testament of her own, dated in 1847, speaks expressly of her brother's will—that, by his will, he had left so-and-so; and the legacies she mentions are to be found in one of the writings on which we are founding. It is thus an unquestionable fact that Mr and Miss Morgan considered and intended those writings to be Mr Morgan's will, and, if we may so say, lived and died in the belief that he was testate. Then there is, finally, the memorandum of 6th September 1846, written by Miss Morgan, and signed by Mr Morgan. Now, this is not a will, but it is such an authentic and solemn expression of purpose, that it is difficult to attribute to it too high qualities as a great corroborative adminicle of the will. These two parties were now the only persons in the world who had any right to or any vital interest in this colossal fortune. It was Mr Morgan's own money, made by his industry and energy, the fruit of his own success in life. The only one now living known to have a drop of his blood in her veins was his sister, Miss Morgan; she had the sole reversionary interest in this fortune. And these two parties—the sole proprietor, and the sole beneficiary—go heart and soul together in this intention of founding an hospital in Dundee; and they record this intention in the most express and explicit terms in the memorandum to which we are now adverting. It is true we cannot make a will to Mr Morgan out of this memorandum, but it will be admitted as the means of explaining and throwing light upon his will; and it will be found to correspond perfectly with the writings on which we have been commenting. (Mr Dodds here mentioned various cases in point). This case, then, is very plain and simple; he had already exhausted all the leading considerations to be kept in view in coming to a decision upon it. Here is Mr Morgan, a native of Dundee, and showing, at various periods of his life, an interest in its welfare, and a kindly feeling to the inhabitants,

Here is he, the sole possessor of a large fortune, tied down by no restraints, fettered by no obligations, having no known kindred but one only sister; and here again is she, the only party having the slightest reversionary interest in the property; we have them both concurring, and mutually cherishing the design of consecrating this fortune to the erection of an educational establishment in their native city. They alone held the arrow in their own hands, to make it speed in whatever direction they choose; and what court in this country do you think will step in and violently turn aside and arrest the intention which Mr Morgan so constantly and seriously entertained, and which, when his whole writings are viewed together, he has declared in a manner not to be misunderstood or denied? It is now a sacred rule in all will cases, that the intention is everything, the form nothing. If he were asked to describe in one word his impression regarding the case, he would say—it was eminently hopeful, and deserved to be taken up and prosecuted on the part of the town. It was not for him to instruct the inhabitants of Dundee what was their duty. He was sure they would come to a wise and useful resolution, and be actuated by the feeling that they were acting in some measure for the whole community, and for posterity. (Loud applause.)

Mr James Brown referred to the terms of the Morgan Settlement, leaving the money to the Nine Trades, a comparatively small body in the town, and asked Mr Dodds if, in the event of these settlements being obtained for Dundee, there would be a probability of the money being available for educational purposes generally amongst the inhabitants, or if it would be confined to the Nine Trades?

Mr Dodds said that it was only in the last deed, the one holograph of Miss Morgan, that the " Nine Trades " were specially referred to. In all the others, those executed by Mr Morgan himself, it was the " town of Dundee " that was specially mentioned. But he had no doubt that were it necessary, either the Court of Session would issue regulations, or a special Act of Parliament could easily be obtained, modernising the purposes of the deeds to the most beneficial purposes.

Mr Brown expressed himself satisfied with the explanation, and moved—

1. " That this meeting have heard with satisfaction the statements now laid before them in regard to the bequest made by the late Mr Morgan, for the erection of an hospital or educational establishment in Dundee.

2. " That, in the opinion of this meeting, it is the duty of the Nine Incorporated Trades, with the support of the Magistrates and Town Council, to take steps for having effect given to the intentions of Mr Morgan.

3. " That the inhabitants of Dundee at large are interested in the right settlement of this question, and should therefore be invited to co-operate with the Town Council and Nine Trades, and also to contribute towards the expenses which may be necessarily incurred in following out the case,

4. "That, for the purpose of aiding the Council and Trades in a matter so important to the community, the following gentlemen be appointed a Committee, with power to add to their number, viz. :— Messrs P. H. Thoms (Convener), James Brown, J. Sturrock, sen., James Neish, James Horsburgh, T. W. Miln, Patrick Anderson, and P. Watson."

Mr John Sturrock seconded the motion, which was carried *nem dis.*

The Provost then moved—"That the thanks of the Meeting be given to Mr Dodds for the very clear and convincing statement made by him, and for the interest he has taken in this matter."

The vote was carried by acclamation, and the thanks of the Meeting having also, on the motion of the Rev. Mr M'Gavin, been accorded to the Provost, the proceedings terminated.

—(From the *Dundee Advertiser.*)

No. IV.

INTERLOCUTORS OF THE COURT OF SESSION.

First Interlocutor of the Lord-Ordinary appealed from, dated May 29, 1857—

" The Lord-Ordinary having heard parties' procurators, and made avizandum, sustains the 2d and 3d pleas in law for the defenders : Assoilzies them from the conclusions of the action, and decerns : Finds the pursuers liable in expenses : allows an account thereof to be given in, and remits to the Auditor to tax the same, when lodged, and to report.

(Signed)   R. HANDYSIDE."

Second Interlocutor appealed from, pronounced by the Second Division of the Court of Session—

" EDINBURGH, *June* 26, 1857.—The Lords having advised the Reclaiming Note for the Magistrates of Dundee, &c., and heard Counsel, adhere to the Interlocutor reclaimed against : Refuse the desire of the Reclaiming Note ; Find the reclaimers liable in additional expenses : and remit to the Auditor to tax and report.

(Signed)   J. HOPE, I.P.D."

No. V.

JUDGMENT OF THE HOUSE OF LORDS ON THE MORGAN BEQUEST, IN FAVOUR OF THE TOWN OF DUNDEE.

DIE MARTIS, 11*th* *May* 1858.

After hearing Counsel, as well on Thursday the 25th, as Friday the 26th, Monday the 29th, and Tuesday the 30th days of March last, upon the Petition and Appeal of John Ewan, present Provost; John Mackay, John Moir, Robert Webster, and Alexander Gilruth, present Bailies; Neil Steel, Treasurer; James Spankie, William Foggie, James Watson, George Welsh, Robert Aitken Mudie, David Heau, Peter Smith, John Ritchie, David Jobson, Andrew Barrie, Andrew John Wighton, David Rollo, Alexander Stuart, and Thomas Cuthbert, present common Councillors of the Royal Burgh of Dundee; and Thomas Smith, present Dean of Guild of the said burgh, all as representing the said burgh and community thereof; and David Hume, baker, Dundee, present Convener, and David Rollo, writer there, present Boxmaster of the Nine Incorporated Trades of Dundee, on behalf of and as representing the said Trades : (which appeal was, by an order of this House, the 15th of March 1858, revived in the names of John Berry of Tayfield, advocate, and David Smith, supervisor of Inland Revenue, residing in Edinburgh, Trustees and Executors of the deceased Mrs Euphan Wanless (or Lyall), relict of Peter Lyall, baker, sometime in Dundee, and thereafter in Edinburgh, one of the respondents, as respondents in the place and stead of the said Mrs Euphan Wanless (or Lyall), deceased, thereto;) complaining of an Interlocutor of the Lords of Session there, of the Second Division, of the 26th of June 1857, and praying that the same might be reversed, varied, or altered, or that the petitioners might have such relief in the premises as to this House in their Lordships' great wisdom should seem meet, as also upon the joint and several answer of John Morris, sometime residing at Saint Thérése de Blainville, near Montreal, Lower Canada, and presently residing in Edinburgh; Mrs Euphan Wanless (or Lyall), now deceased, lately residing in Edinburgh, relict of Peter Lyall, baker, sometime in Dundee, and thereafter in Edinburgh; and Mrs Ann Wanless (or Duncan), wife of Robert Duncan, gardener at Parknowe, near Newport, Fife, and presently residing there; Mrs Allison Wanless (or Ritchie), wife of George Ritchie, quarryman at Mylnefield or Kingoodie Quarry, near Dundee, and presently residing at Mylnefield or Kingoodie Quarry aforesaid; and William Morris, farmer, township of Albion, in Canada West, all next of kin and representatives of the deceased John Morgan, sometime residing in Coates Crescent, Edinburgh; and the said Robert Duncan and George Ritchie, and the said John Morris, mandatory for the said William Morris, put into the said appeal, and which said appeal was, by an order of this House of the 4th of February last, heard *ex parte* as to Alexander

Morgan, and James Morgan, and Donald Lindsay, they not having answered the said appeal though peremptorily ordered so to do, and due consideration had this day of what was offered on either side in this cause : It is ordered and adjudged by the Lords spiritual and temporal in Parliament assembled, That the said interlocutor complained of in the said appeal, be and the same are hereby reversed ; and it is further ordered that the said respondents do repay to the said appellants the expenses to which the said respondents were found entitled by the said interlocutors appealed from if they shall have been paid by the said appellants : and it is further ordered that the costs in respect of this appeal incurred by the said appellants, and by such of the respondents as have answered the appeal, be paid out of the estate, the subject of this appeal, the amount of such costs to be certified by the clerk of the Parliaments : and it is declared that the testamentary writings left by the deceased John Morgan, and in the condescendence annexed to the summons mentioned, contain a valid legacy and bequest of so much of the personal estate of the said testator, John Morgan, as is necessary to found an hospital in the town of Dundee to accommodate one hundred boys : and it is further ordered that the Court of Session do make such interlocutors and orders and give such directions as shall be necessary for the purposes following ; that is to say, for framing a scheme for establishing, in the town of Dundee, an hospital to contain one hundred boys, and lodging, maintaining, and educating them therein, in fulfilment of the testamentary bequest and intention of the said testator ; and for enquiring into and ascertaining the amount of the estate of the said testator necessary for carrying into effect such scheme, and for applying the same accordingly, and also for adjudicating upon the expenses incurred in the Court below : and it is also further ordered that the cause be and is hereby remitted back to the Court of Session in Scotland to do and proceed further therein as shall be just and consistent with this declaration, and these directions, and this judgment.

(Signed)   JOHN GEORGE SHAW LEFEVRE,

Cler. Parliamentarian.

Counsel for the Appellants—Messrs Rolt, Q.C. ; James Anderson, Q.C. ; and George H. Thoms, Advocate.

Agents in London—Messrs Dodds & Greig, Westminster ; in Scotland—Mr John Rogers, S.S.C., Edinburgh, and Mr David Rollo, Dundee.

Counsel for the Respondents—The Lord Advocate, the Solicitor-General of England, and Mr Roundell Palmer.

Agents in London—Messrs Richardson, Loch, & Maclaurin ; in Scotland—Messrs Webster & Black, S.S.C., and Messrs Adam & Kirk, W.S., Edinburgh.

No. VI.

REPORT OF A PUBLIC MEETING HELD ON THE 17TH MAY 1858.

A public meeting of the subscribers to the fund for trying the Morgan Case, was held in the Town Hall yesterday, at two o'clock. The meeting was numerously attended, and Provost Rollo occupied the chair.

Provost Rollo congratulated the subscribers on the decision which had been pronounced in favour of the town in the Morgan Case, and read the remarks made in the House of Lords regarding the costs which they would receive out of the estate.

Mr P. H. Thoms concurred with Provost Rollo in his congratulations as to the pleasing result of the action, and gave a clear and able statement of the various steps which had been taken by the town in regard to it since the death of Mr Morgan. As some remarks had been made by Counsel in the House of Lords tending to throw blame on the Magistrates of Dundee for unnecessary delay in instituting their action, Mr Thoms, in the course of his observations, quoted the opinion given by the Lord-President of the Court of Session and Lord Neaves on the 12th December 1850.

Mr John Sturrock thought the town of Dundee was much indebted to Provost Thoms for the assiduity and intelligence with which he had all along engaged in this matter. He thought they should now appoint a small Committee to consider the whole matter, and watch the case in the Court of Session, with a view of obtaining the most beneficial application of the funds.

Mr Rough thought they should now pass a cordial vote of thanks to Provost Thoms for his able and zealous management of this case from first to last. He also thought they were much indebted to Mr Dodds, of London, and to Mr Thoms, advocate, for the able manner in which they had all along attended to the interests of the town in this case. Mr Rough concluded by proposing the following motion:—

"That this meeting desires to record the high sense of the important services rendered to the community by ex-Provost Thoms in reference to the action which has now been decided by the judgment of the House of Lords. It was chiefly through Mr Thoms that the claims of the town were first brought into public notice; and the views which he has from the first entertained as to the prospect of ultimate success have been fully justified by the result. To his personal exertions it was in a great measure owing that subscriptions were obtained to meet the expense of carrying on the proceedings; and from first to last he has watched the case with the deepest and most intelligent interest. The meeting, while thus giving expression to their own feelings, have reason to believe that they faithfully represent the sentiments entertained by the community at large."

The vote of thanks to Mr P. H. Thoms was carried by acclamation, and it was also agreed to record a vote to Mr Dodds, and Mr Thoms, advocate, and also to Mr George Duncan, for the trouble he had taken in the case when Member for the Burgh.

Mr P. H. Thoms, in returning thanks for the compliment, said he would be amply rewarded for his trouble in the Morgan Case by the thought that the youth of Dundee would enjoy the benefits of a valuable educational institution when he and all those around him were sleeping in the grave.

Mr George Duncan, in a few remarks, testified to the trouble taken in this case by Mr P. H. Thoms, Mr Dodds, and Mr Thoms, advocate.

Mr P. H. Thoms intimated that there was still a balance of £360 at the credit of the subscribers in the bank, after paying the Court of Session expenses, and the expenses necessary in preparing for the appeal to the House of Lords.

The Committee formerly appointed by the subscribers to carry on the action was re-appointed to watch over the case when it came back to the Court of Session, Mr Rough's name being substituted for that of Mr James Brown, and Mr Hume's being added to the list. The Committee was instructed to co-operate with the Committees that might be appointed by the Town Council and the Nine Trades.

The proceedings terminated with a vote of thanks to Provost Rollo.

—(*Dundee Advertiser*, 18th May 1858.)

No. VII.

Inscriptions on Sepulchral Monuments.

Inscription on Monument in the Old Burying Ground, Dundee.

" Erected
To the Memory of
Euphemia Dacres
Mother to the undermentioned Thomas Morgan ;
Thomas Morgan,
Aged 75 years ;
Robert Morgan, Helen Morgan,
and
Janet Morgan,
Children of the said Thomas Morgan
and
Janet Cramond.

This Monument was erected by
John Morgan,
Second and only surviving son of the above-named Thomas
Morgan and Janet Cramond.
September 1st 1817."

Inscription on Monument erected in Greyfriar's Churchyard, Edinburgh.

"THOMAS MORGAN, Esq., died at Haddington,
13th August 1815,
late of the
Bengal Medical Establishment;
also
Mrs JANET MORGAN,
who died at Edinburgh
on the 14th October 1818,
Aged 85 Years and 9 Months,
Mother to the above Mr Thomas Morgan;
also
Miss MATILDA MORGAN,
died on 20th March 1827,
Daughter of the above Mrs Janet Morgan.
Miss AGNES MORGAN,
died 15th January 1848, aged 67.
JOHN MORGAN, Esq.,
died at 17 Coates Crescent, Edinburgh,
25th August 1850. Aged 90.

THOMAS MORGAN died August 1799."

No. VIII.

EXTRACTS FROM OBSERVATIONS ON HIS FAMILY CONNECTIONS, IN THE HANDWRITING OF MR MORGAN.

Agnes Gall, a cousin of John Morgan of the Wallace of Craigie, and grandfather to J. M. Agnes Gall's grandfather was married to Ogilvie of Carsebank, daughter of Ogilvie of Carsebank in Forfarshire, barony of Rescobie, and town and lands of Aberlemno. Agnes Gall was the mother of the present Mr Maule, minister of Monikie, whose ancestors came from East Lothian, and supposed a descendant of William Maul, Archdeacon of Lothian, who was a brother of Sir Patrick Maule of Panmure (See Nisbet's Heraldry). It is reported that the late and last Earl of Panmure recognised a female of the name of Morgan, who was his house-keeper, as one of his relatives.

"The tradition is by another part of the family of Morgans, that they are originally from Germany and France. (This is of a very late date, and supposed to have been one of the Morgans or Mackays that went to Bohemia in Charles I.'s time, but their origin in Scotland must have been in King Lear's time.) At the conquest in 1130, or in 1260 from England or Wales,—in Glenesk in Forfarshire 1296, Morgan signed his fealty to Edward I. of England. They bring in support of this, armorial bearings transmitted to them by a Dr William Morgan, who was in Paris about 1740 or 1745, that he was recognised as of the same family by a General William Morgan, then in the service of France, who said he was born in Britain, but that his father was a resident in France, although their ancestors were originally from Germany. These armorial bearings have a strong resemblance to the Mackays, the present Lord Reay; if so, the Mackays are the descendants of, or, as described by Wood and Playfair, from Magnus, the Father of Morgan, a military ruler in 1165 at Caithness, &c. In the Irish language that is Mortadgore; and in English it is Morgan. It is reasonable to suppose (if the Morgans are not time immemorial residents in Germany, and they must have been long established in that country by the left-hand marriages having acquired the name of the Morganic marriage, which is only peculiar to Germany) to be the descendants of the Mackays, who went to Bohemia in the time of Charles I. of England.

" N.B.—As the Mauls came into Scotland at 1130, this is more likely to agree with the tradition of the Morgans having come with the Mauls from England, say rather than from France, especially as the tradition in the Mackay's family is, that they came about the end of the twelfth century, and the original name of the Mackays was Morgan."

No. IX.

LETTERS.

Letter from John Morgan, Esq., to J. Hanley, Esq., dated Edinburgh, 3d November 1818.

" SIR,—In consequence of your advertisement in the *Courier* newspaper, I beg leave to trouble you with annexed copy of my letter to Mr Morgan, Procureur-General, Amiens, on 15th January last. I wish to know if M. M. received this letter, and if he can satisfactorily answer the queries therein contained.

" You'll be pleased to address me at Queen Street, Edinburgh, N.B., as soon as your leisure will admit of, and at same time inform me what I shall be indebted to you for this trouble, and to whom I am to pay the amount.

Despatched 3d November, by post.

Letter to Monsieur Morgan, Procureur-General, Amiens.

" Edinburgh, 15th January 1818.—Permit me to request the favour of you to examine the enclosed armorial bearings, which I presume to do in consequence of the similarity of name. At same time will you have the goodness to endeavour to obtain an explanation of the inscription on these armorial bearings which belonged to a General William Morgan, who was in the French service during the years 1745-1746.

"My relation, Dr William Morgan, and the said General William Morgan, recognised each other as relatives—the General representing himself as having been born in Britain, his father as a resident in France, although his family were originally from Germany. I shall be infinitely obliged to you when the more important duties of your high office will admit of a reply, to notice if any of the relatives of General William Morgan and of Dr William Morgan are alive—the country.from which the General's family originally came, and the explanation of the motto on these armorial bearings. None of the antiquarians in Edinburgh, or Sir Isaac Heard, Garter of the College of Arms in London, could explain the inscription, or even guess at the character it is written in.

"About the month of August last I had the armorial bearings transmitted to Messrs Vassal & Coy., in Paris, to procure an explanation, as well as to obtain information respecting General William Morgan and Dr William Morgan ; but I have not yet received any satisfactory account of either, which is the cause of my presuming to trouble you."

Letter from John Morgan, Esq., to Sir W. Houston, 2d July (year blank).

"To Sir Wm. Houston, K.G.C., &c. &c.,
         "At Ausford, *via* Arundel, Sussex.

"MY DEAR SIR,—I have to acknowledge the receipt of your favour of the 28th ult., and regret that I cannot give you any account about Helen Morgan ; but if you'll oblige me with any information that may tend to find out her representatives, I will apply to the commissary sheriff, and the other registers for information on this subject. I have been many years employed on a similar search, and found all the records sadly mutilated from the rebellions in 1715 and 1745, and the parochial registers carelessly kept. My object was to trace back my descent from the Morgans of Glenesk, in Forfarshire, who swore fealty to Edward the First when he overran Scotland in 1296.

"It is with no small pleasure we learn that Lady Jean has received great benefit from the Buxton waters, which we earnestly wish they may so continue to do, and have the happy effect of restoring her to her wonted health.

"I presume if Lady Jean can acquire additional strength for the voyage, that the warm climate will expel the enemy. Pray, does Miss Long attend you to Gibraltar ?

"My sister unites me in wishing you and all the family everything that is good.
                    "I am, &c."

No. X.

Extract from Second Report by ARCHIBALD CAMPBELL SWINTON, Esq., *in Declarator,* THE MAGISTRATES AND NINE INCORPORATED TRADES OF DUNDEE, *against* JOHN MORRIS, *and others.*

The Reporter submits the following—

AMENDED ESTIMATE OF EXPENDITURE.

1. Feu-duty per annum, being for three acres instead of two, as formerly proposed,	£60	0	0
2. Head-Master, - - - -	200	0	0
3. Second Master, instead of £100, formerly proposed,	90	0	0
4. Third Master, instead of £80, formerly proposed,	70	0	0
5. Occasional tuition, - - - -	50	0	0
6. Matron, instead of £50, formerly proposed, -	45	0	0
7. Physician, - - - - -	25	0	0
8. Treasurer and Clerk, - - -	60	0	0
9. Auditor, - - - - -	10	10	0
10. Servants, - - - - -	94	0	0
11. Janitor and Gardener, - - -	40	0	0
12. Housekeeping, instead of £840, formerly proposed,	800	0	0
13. Clothing, instead of £400, formerly proposed, -	383	15	0
14. Books and Stationary, instead of £50, formerly proposed, - - - - -	40	0	0
15. Fire and light, - - - -	90	0	0
16. Repairs, - - - - -	40	0	0
17. Taxes, - - - - -	30	0	0
18. Fire insurance, - - - -	14	8	0
19. Church seats, - - - -	12	10	0
20. Extra expenses, such as duplicand of feu-duty, travelling charges of Visitors and Inspector, printing and advertising, sickbed and funeral expenses of boys, retiring allowances for Masters, and general Incidents, - -	112	0	0
	£2,267	3	0

Assuming, according to the first part of this Report, that interest is to be at 3½ per cent., the capital sum required, in order to produce the above annual income of £2,267, 3s. is   -   £64,775 14   3

Add to which the estimated cost of buildings and furniture, as stated in the Report formerly submitted
to the Court, -   -   -   £13,503   0   0

And the additional cost in enclosing
walls and laying out ground, occa-
sioned by 3 acres being taken instead
of 2,   -   -   -   150   0   0

                                              13,653   0   0

               Total sum required,   -   £78,428 14   3

Supposing the site to be immediately acquired, and building opera-
tions commenced, the funds which will be required before the Hospital
is completed, will be as follows:—

At the commencement, say,   -   -   -   £3,375   0   0

At the end of the first year, the second instalment
for the building, and relative expenses, say,   -   6,875   0   0

At the end of the second year, when the building
is presumed to be finished,   -   -   -   3,500   0   0

The Hospital is supposed to be opened partially at the end of the
second year, when the income from £42,000, viz., £1,470 is held to be
required. A farther admission of pupils is supposed to take place at
the end of the third year, when the income from £13,000 additional,
viz., £455, will be required, and at the end of the fourth year, when
the full numbers are supposed to be admitted into the Hospital, the
remainder of the capital will be required, viz., £9,678, 14s. 3d.

Till the end of this period of four years, the funds are supposed to
be yielding interest at 3 per cent., and, accordingly, the Reporter has
discounted the whole at that rate.

View of the present value of the Estimated Funds on the above data.

	Value when required.	Discount.	Present amount required.
Sum to be reserved for imme-diate requirements, ...	£3,375 0 0	...	£3,375 0 0
Value of Second Instalment for the buildings required at end of the *first* year,.................	6,875 0 0	£200 4 10	6,674 15 2
Last Instalment required at end of *second* year, ...	3,500 0 0	200 18 4	3,299 1 8
Sum required for Hospital pur-poses at the end of *second* year, ...	42,000 0 0	2,410 19 5	39,589 0 7
Sum required for additional Hospital purposes at end of *third* year,........................	13,000 0 0	1,103 3 2	11,896 16 10
Balance required at end of *fourth* year,......................	9,678 14 3	1,079 6 0	8,599 8 3
	£78,428 14 3	£4,994 11 9	£73,434 2 6

It thus appears that for the Erection and Endowment of the Morgan Hospital, according to the estimate recommended by the Reporter for adoption, the sum which it is necessary should be at once laid aside for investment is £73,434, 2s. 6d., say £73,500. And it must be kept in view that the money itself will be required for the purposes of the Hospital, not the equivalent value in Government stock or other security which may be subject to fluctuation.

No. XI.

DESCRIPTION OF THE BUILDING.

The following description of the building, planned by Messrs Peddie & Kinnear, of Edinburgh, is from the pen of a gentleman intimately acquainted with the plans which have been prepared. The designs prepared by Messrs Peddie & Kinnear will, by their ornamental and effective character, do ample justice to the site. It is only of modern date that Dundee possesses almost any architectural attractions, but from time to time some of its fine natural features have been filled up with buildings of considerable pretensions. But in the east of the town it is entirely blank in the element of decorative architecture, and some embellishment is much needed to relieve the dull character of the factory buildings which are now encroaching upon this elevated ground. The new Hospital, keeping entirely clear of this heavy and uninviting group, will present a lively and cheerful feature in the more open part of the landscape. The ground obtained for the building is nearly triangular, and forms a sort of gushet between the Forfar road going north and the old Arbroath road breaking off to the north-east. The gateway is at the junction of the two roads, and the enclosure walls extend about 250 yards along each road, the divergent lines being united by a wall of about 150 yards, forming the top of the inverted triangle. The ground enclosed measures about five acres. It slopes upwards from the entrance gate, and the Hospital will be built in the upper and broader portion of the grounds. The design presents a building quadrangular in form, 200 feet in breadth, 120 feet in depth, with an open court inside. The building is French (or Flemish) Gothic in character, and is two storeys in height, with a centre tower rising to the height of 120 feet. The tower, the body of which is 20 feet square, projects a few feet from the façade. In the ground floor it contains the main doorway, which is formed in a richly moulded and carved archway, surmounted by a croqueted label. Over the doorway in the second storey is a three-light window, headed with cinquefoil tracery, and opening into a projecting balcony. On reaching the height of the ridge of the building—the intervening space being filled in by a block—the tower is corbelled out in the angles into circular turrets, each capped with a steep slated roof, finished by an ornamental vane. Connecting the turrets are carved balconies, also corbelled out from the main walls of the tower. From this point the tower rises in a steep roof, formed in two stages, and exhibits in front a richly carved group of windows, surmounted by an ornamental gablet. The tower terminates in double pinnacles, united by an ornamental crest. On each side of the tower the design exhibits handsome bay windows in the second storey, surmounted by steep, crow-step gables. Extending on either side is a range of two-light windows in both storeys, the upper being finished by gablets flanked and terminated by pinnacles. At the angles of the front the building throws out slightly projecting wings, with a triple square-headed window in the lower storey, and with two traceried windows in the upper storey, separated by a projecting ornamental chimney shaft, which terminates in a crow-step gable. The gables of both wings are flanked by buttresses surmounted by shafts terminating in carved pinnacles. The roof is of high pitch, and is finished by an elaborate iron chest. The groups of tall chimney-stacks, rising at intervals from the roof, form an effective and characteristic feature of the design. The east elevation is of the same general character as the front, and is broken in the centre by two projecting gables, to the north of which is a section of the building, containing the dining-hall on the ground floor, and the chapel in the upper floor. The chapel is marked by pointed and traceried windows, rising in beautifully finished gablets, and from the roof springs an airy bell tower, rising thirty-two feet above the ridge of the roof. In the west elevation the leading feature is the staircase tower, which rises to the height of eighty feet. The tower exhibits a steep slated roof, broken with dormer windows, terminating in a double finial and carved rail. To the north of this tower is the Head-Master's residence, which, in somewhat plainer style, preserves the general features of the building. The north elevation shows the end of the chapel in a three-light window, with geometrical tracery, with a cross surmounting the gable. The rest of the north elevation is filled up by the Kitchen and Offices, extending towards the north-west angle, in which the Head-Master's house is situated. The open Court, which lights the building from the interior, is about 130 feet by 50. With regard to the internal arrangements of the building, we may state generally that, in entering by the main doorway, we find on the left the Board Room, the Library Clerk's Room, and Matron's Apartments; and on the right, the Master's and Matron's Dining-Rooms, and a series of large Class-Rooms, extending towards the Dining-Hall. In the upper floor are five well-aired dormitories, with a properly separated Infirmary in the west wing, as also Lavatories

and Bath-Room. On both floors the ceilings are about fifteen feet high. There are also apartments in the tower which may be put to useful services, and from the windows of which a magnificent prospect will be obtained. The total cost of the building, including gates, lodges, and enclosure walls, and a separate building for workshops in rear of the main structure, will be about £15,000.
—*Dundee Advertiser*, 31st July 1863.

PRINTED BY JAMES P. MATHEW AND CO., MEADOWSIDE, DUNDEE.